# SHILTON
# ON GOALKEEPING

# SHILTON ON GOALKEEPING

## PETER SHILTON

HEADLINE

Peter Shilton © 1992

The right of Peter Shilton to be identified as author of
the work has been asserted by him in accordance with the
Copyright, Designs and Patents Act 1988

First published in 1992
by HEADLINE BOOK PUBLISHING PLC

10 9 8 7 6 5 4 3 2 1

British Library Cataloguing in Publication Data
Shilton, Peter
Shilton on Goalkeeping
I. Title.
796.334

0-7472-0718-6

Designed by Peter Champion
Illustrations by Hardlines

Photoset in North Wales by
Derek Doyle & Associates, Mold, Clwyd

Illustrations reproduced by
Koford, Singapore

Printed and bound in Great Britain by
Butler & Tanner Limited, Frome

HEADLINE BOOK PUBLISHING PLC
Headline House
79 Great Titchfield Street
London W1P 7FN

# CONTENTS

# INTRODUCTION

There is a saying in football that you don't win a First Division Championship without a good goalkeeper. That shows how important a keeper is to a team. To win the title a club has to be consistent throughout the season – and that applies to the goalkeeper more than any other member of the side. It is a position where you need someone who is dependable, reliable and who does not make too many mistakes. A goalie often has to play extremely well when the team are struggling to find their top form. If an outfield player has an off day, at least there are nine others to offer support and fill the gaps. If a keeper is off form and makes mistakes, then he will give away goals and will receive hostile treatment from the terraces and the press. Goalkeeping errors cost goals and valuable points.

Goalkeeping is a one-off position for the obvious reason that the keeper is the only man on the pitch who can use his hands. In that sense, he is a unique player with separate individual needs, but at the same time he is always looked on as part of the team. However, it is only in recent years that managers have started to develop their appreciation of the art of goalkeeping and many ex-keepers are now employed as coaches to pass on their highly specialised craft. I am glad to see that more managers and coaches are now aware that it is a unique position, with special needs for training and coaching. In this book we demonstrate that goalkeeping is a specialist position that requires many different skills. I have always said that you need greater all-round ability to play in goal than in any outfield position. A goalie needs the nimbleness and agility of a gymnast, the resilience of a rugby forward and the handling skills of a basketball player.

Another popular old adage is that you have to be crazy to be a keeper. This is basically because a goalkeeper is usually more of an individualist. The man in the number one jersey tends to be slightly different from the rest of the team in terms of personality. You need certain attributes to stand between the sticks and be shot at or to dive at the flying feet of a forward! Furthermore, goalkeepers are singled out for criticism more than any other player and must be able to take it.

Goalkeepers also need a good sense of humour and have to be able to retain their confidence when goals go past them or when they make crucial errors. I have found that a game of football can be completely different from week to week for a keeper in a way that can never be the same for outfield players. Sometimes you have to stand throughout a whole match with little or nothing to do, and then the next game you face a 90-minute bombardment when your team is under continual pressure from the opposition. In my experience, many different characters, with varying approaches to the game, play in goal; some are very forceful and

PREVIOUS PAGE: I had to sit out my first game as player/manager at Plymouth because the opposition was the club I'd just left – Derby.

aggressive, others have a quiet disposition. You have to be different to want to be the odd man out in a team. That may explain why so many claim that goalkeepers are crazy.

There's no doubt that soccer's biggest personalities wear the number one jersey. Keepers are always likely to provide some eccentric behaviour on the field.

Bruce Grobbelaar is looked upon as the clown prince of soccer and has a great rapport with the crowd. He's quite capable of any antics on the pitch, as well as pulling off miraculous saves. Bruce has worn funny hats, performed handstands when Liverpool have scored and gave his famous wobbly legs act to put off an Italian penalty-taker in a European Cup-tie. Bruce probably comes further off his line than just about any other keeper.

Bruce Grobbelaar, one of the great goalkeeping extroverts, celebrates a Liverpool goal in inimitable fashion.

John 'Budgie' Burridge is a good friend who modelled himself on me in the early stages of his career. He is another veteran goalkeeper who is still playing, thanks to his dedication and total obsession with the game. 'Budgie' is a fitness fanatic and he used to come onto the pitch before kick-off and do gymnastics and somersaults. The crowd always enjoyed the show.

At one time I could never understand why Leeds' Welsh international keeper Gary Sprake, chewed so much gum – his jaws must have ached after 90 minutes. Chewing-gum wrappers were littered all around his goal. That was because, before the days of specialist gloves, Sprake used to stick gum on his hands to help his grip. He gave a very sticky handshake at the end of the game!

Another Welsh international star, Neville Southall, is also one of the game's great characters. He sometimes looks as if he's played for 90 minutes before a ball's been kicked in anger. Neville often dives around so much in warming up, that he's covered in mud before the match begins. In appearance, Neville is one of the most distinctive goalies in the game. He always has his socks rolled down, displaying his pads and a shirt collar sticking up under his jersey. He also coats his eyebrows in enormous quantities of Vaseline.

Just about the most crazy keeper of recent years must undoubtedly be Colombian international Réné Higuita. He's the goalie with the reputation for coming out of his box to join in moves. I have seen him dribble down the wing and tackle an opponent on the half-way line. He is the ultimate in sweeper-keepers. He did come unstuck, though, against Cameroon in the World Cup when he came out of his penalty area and lost the ball to Roger Milla, who went on to score.

Jean-Marie Pfaff of Belgium was another international goalkeeping personality. We played for a half each in a match for the Rest of the World against New York Cosmos. Fifty yards behind the goal was a group of cheerleaders. After we scored, he left his goal and joined in with them for the celebrations. Suddenly, the Cosmos launched an attack and Pfaff had to race back to get on his goal line in time.

Goalkeeper is the most enjoyable position to play, as when you get everything right and do well, everybody appreciates your work. Everyone will notice when you come and catch crosses or make good saves. They will see if you are brave and your anticipation is good. There is no greater reward than stopping the opposition from scoring and having a feeling of invincibility. At these times, you know your skills are in tip-top condition. It is a wonderful feeling to know that the other team cannot beat you with a shot or cross.

Good preparation for matches will heighten your enjoyment. If you train well, then you go onto the pitch feeling confident about every part of your game. Whatever the opposition try, you're keen to deal with any attack. Some teams may pepper you with shots. On another day you may have to catch a succession of crosses. At other times you will have to respond to a series of through balls. One of the exciting aspects of goalkeeping is that you can never know how you will have to play before a match and what part of your game you will need to excel at. If you have trained hard and prepared well, then you will be ready to meet any challenge.

The exhilaration of goalkeeping comes from knowing exactly what you are doing and being confident of combatting any situation. Some keepers do not gain as much enjoyment from playing as they should, because they are strong at some skills of the game and weak at others. When they are faced with a situation they are not good at dealing with, they become frustrated and either grow angry or apprehensive. That takes away some of the pleasure and can cause friction with the defenders. Nobody likes to let goals in, but sometimes you cannot do anything to stop someone scoring. When you have done all you can to save a shot and it has still gone in, then you derive some satisfaction from making it hard for your opponent.

Réné Higuita, Colombia's sweeper-keeper, takes on the Yugoslav attack during the 1990 World Cup.

It is important for a keeper to train harder than an outfield player, as he has a wider range of skills to practise. A goalie has to prepare well for a game as he has to be alert for the full 90 minutes. He may be over-worked or have one shot to save. He must always be on his toes as at any stage a player, whether in a Sunday park match or a World Cup final, can produce an unstoppable shot out of the blue.

Another great advantage with taking up the number one job in football is that one can have a much longer playing career. Keepers like Dino Zoff of Italy, Pat Jennings of Northern Ireland and myself have played international football in our 40s. These days, that would be almost impossible in any other position on the field. I have also seen many goalkeepers of a ripe old age playing in local leagues and Sunday soccer. Experience and positional sense can more than compensate for slowing reactions and advancing years. Although goalkeepers tend to play on a bit longer, that may be balanced in part by the fact that their apprenticeship is usually longer and harder. Unlike outfield players, a keeper doesn't usually reach his peak until he is about 30 years old, and many are at the height of their powers in their mid-30s. During this period a goalkeeper has an ideal mixture of experience and athleticism.

This book sets out to emphasise that every facet of goalkeeping needs constant practice and assessment. It is important to understand that you need to have good all-round skills and no real weaknesses to play in goal. You have to attempt to master all the different techniques of goalkeeping. All aspects of the job will be covered in this book, with a series of exercises to help you. They are designed to be enjoyable, as well as being essential in developing your skills. At the very least, they will give you a base from which to start your training. You can build on these exercises and even develop your own to help you become a top goalkeeper. I encourage all youngsters to try to invent their own movements to aid their agility.

This book will explain all the essential techniques for stopping shots and catching crosses. We look at basic skills like narrowing the angle, getting the body behind the ball, catching at the highest point, and when to catch or punch. We also look at distribution, how to deal with penalty kicks and the way a keeper should marshall his defence. There is also a chapter to help young players and their parents to choose the correct kit for keeping.

Although our football in Britain seems to come under constant criticism from the press and the public, nobody can doubt the fact that these islands have always had the highest standards of goalkeeping in world soccer. I am proud to have set a record of 125 international caps for a keeper, following in the tradition of great keepers in the UK. We have a heritage of goalkeepers like Frank Swift, Bert Williams, Gordon Banks, Pat Jennings and Neville Southall who have been the envy of other countries. I hope that better coaching and instruction will help to uphold this reputation.

For this book I have put together all the techniques and 'tricks of the trade' that I've gathered in over 25 years of playing top-class football, as well as my experiences in internationals and three World Cups. If you are a goalkeeper, then you should be proud to be a member of sport's most exclusive club. Goalies are number one in a soccer team and that is precisely what goalkeeping is – the number one job in football. There have been few instructional books on goalkeeping and not enough specialised coaching. I hope this guide will encourage you to wear the coveted number one jersey and serve as an introduction to the position – and take you all the way to the England team!

# GOALKEEPING

I gained my first experience as a goalkeeper at primary school. I then progressed through local representative soccer and an early association with my home town club, Leicester City. I graduated as a goalkeeper when I signed on for them as a professional. Many factors combined to guide me as a keeper and shape my career in soccer. As with any professional sportsman, I have suffered setbacks and enjoyed successes in my career. It is by relating my own personal experiences that I can give an insight into what it takes to become a top-class keeper and to pass on some of the knowledge gained along the way. Everyone has a different approach to the game, but my development was helped by several people who gave me good advice. Above all, talent is not enough without hard work and dedication to back it up.

My first memory of playing football was when I was at primary school and I can recall very clearly my days at Court Crescent Junior School in Leicester. It was at the age of eight that I first became a football fanatic. We used to have an hour or so during an afternoon called 'Sports Time' when we would have a game of football on a small patch of grass at the back of the school building. Like many youngsters the world over, we used to put down coats or bibs to mark out the goals. At that time, I used to play out on the pitch, but I do remember that I occasionally used to go in goal. We were also fortunate to have a park on the other side of the road from the school. When the evenings started to grow longer in March, we used to go onto the recreation ground for half an hour or an hour's practice before we went home. At the age of nine or ten, that was my first serious practice as a soccer player.

Those sessions on the park were a lot of fun and helped to develop my skills. At the time, I received much encouragement from my family. My mum, dad and elder brother were all keen to see me play soccer. My father, Les, ran a greengrocery business and used to work on Saturday mornings, but he always used to stop off for a few minutes when he was making deliveries around our estate to watch me play. I will always remember him pulling up in the van and standing on the touchline wearing his white working clothes. He never missed watching me. He was a great encouragement to me at that early age. However hard he was working, he would manage to spare some time to come along to my matches. Although I wasn't spoilt, my parents made sure I got a good football or some soccer kit every birthday or Christmas. We certainly weren't a rich family, but I was always well looked after. I always had the kit and equipment I needed and owe my start in soccer to my parents. Family backing and encouragement are essential for an aspiring sports star.

I must confess I don't really know why I chose to go in goal.

PREVIOUS PAGE: One of the highlights of my club career came when Nottingham Forest beat Hamburg 1-0 in the European Cup final of 1980. Garry Birtles joins me in a lap of honour in Madrid.

Perhaps some inner sense guided me and told me that that was the position to play. I did very much enjoy goalkeeping from about the age of eight onwards, and I think I liked the fact that a goalkeeper was very much an individual within the team. One of the immediate pleasures was diving around and making good stops and saves. As a youngster, I liked the competitive element of being a keeper, the direct confrontation of someone trying to beat me. It is similar to a boxer who doesn't like to be knocked over or hurt. A goalkeeper doesn't like to be beaten or have the ball put past him. All keepers gain great enjoyment from stopping the opposition scoring and I found the position very fascinating at an early age.

When I was 11, I would come home and do drawings of practice and training routines. I would also draw diagrams to work out the sort of angles I should be taking to stop shots and cut out crosses. Then I'd take my studies down to the park and get my friends to help me put them into practice. Instead of just kicking the ball around and shooting, I would work on certain disciplines to attempt to improve my skills. You should not think that because you are still young you cannot work constructively on your game. I always enjoyed these sessions because I felt a great urge to play football and was never as happy as when I was playing. I think I had withdrawal symptoms at the age of 11 and 12 if I went a few days without a game. It was almost impossible to satisfy my appetite for football.

When I wasn't playing I was practising. Next door to my father's greengrocer's shop we used to have a big wall. After I had finished school and had a kick around on the park, I used to come home and practise by knocking the ball against the wall. A nearby street-lamp provided adequate floodlighting. One point I must stress to all schoolboy soccer players is that I did make sure I did all my homework as well. Any spare time other than that was spent playing soccer. I would have played out in the street in the pitch dark if my parents had let me, as I wanted to do everything I could to develop my craft.

As I grew up I joined a boys' club. The activities kept me busy and also helped me to train and practise my goalkeeping. I got my first big chance when I was 11 years old. Schoolboys in Leicestershire were invited to come down to Leicester City Football Club for a series of tests that were judged by the club's coaches. They invited me to come down to Filbert Street for training twice a week with the amateurs and semi-professionals. They gave me some very valuable coaching and advice for four years before I signed on as an apprentice at the club. Perhaps I was lucky to be invited for the coaching tests and to be noticed at that early age.

There was a time when I thought I was going to be too small to be in goal, so I played in the outfield as well. If I was going to be too short to be a keeper, I wanted to have the extra option of being able to play in other positions. To try to increase my height I carried out a lot of stretching exercises. Some of the things I tried may seem ridiculous: I used to hang on to the bannisters at home, with my parents holding on to my ankles; I also used to do stretching exercises up the wall. Anything to make me bigger. My mother used to make sure I ate well and had plenty of good food. There are so many different theories about diets for sportspeople these days. I used to consume a lot of steak and salad and drink milk to help build myself up. Whether the stretching exercises and the diet really did me any good I'll never know, but I did start to shoot up when I was 12 or 13, and from then on I knew goalkeeping was my position. I must add that I was so mad keen on football, I would have tried to be an outfield player had I not been big enough to fill the keeper's jersey.

One fact I deal with later in the book is that young goalkeepers have great difficulties in coping with crosses. This is because, in schoolboy football, a goalie's main activity is dealing with shots on goal, as not many boys have the strength or power to cross the ball right into the middle of the goalmouth. That was certainly the case when I played schoolboy soccer. This means that keepers cannot practise the technique regularly and so may struggle when first up against older players. However, while some skills need a lot of developing, I found that most aspects of goalkeeping did come fairly naturally to me.

One of my most enjoyable memories was playing for my primary school team. On Fridays we waited in anticipation for the school side to be announced. I remember we had to pick up our kit from school. The keeper's jersey was very different to the style worn today. It was a roll-necked pullover made of wool. It really was a big thrill to be picked for the team and a disappointment for the lads who were left out. On a Friday night I used to go home and conscientiously clean my boots. I even used to wash the laces to make my footwear immaculate. It was exciting to wake up on the Saturday morning to go down and meet the other members of the team at school. We either had to travel to play at another school or carry the posts to and from the nearby park. At that age, it wasn't a chore, but part of the enjoyment and a time I'll never forget. I firmly believe that putting up posts and nets, helping to mark the pitch and prepare the kit helps give youngsters a greater appreciation of the game.

My first experience of a local derby was at primary school. The big match in those days was Court Crescent versus Braunstone Hall. The two schools were just half a mile apart. It was a bit like

The Leicester Boys team of 1959/60, with me in the middle of the back row.

a junior version of Liverpool against Everton: while the Merseyside teams are separated by Stanley Park, we were separated by Leicester's Braunstone Park. They were the first 'needle' matches I had taken part in. We used to play during the lighter evenings after school. For a junior school game, there was always a big crowd of locals watching. The matches were very even. It was a great triumph to beat the school from the other side of the park, but very deflating if we lost.

The next stage in my career was to try to play in representative teams. In Leicester there were many different area school teams. I found that every time I achieved something, I wanted to take another step up the ladder to an eventual professional career. From the school team I moved up to the local XI and finally gained selection for the Leicester Boys side.

I mentioned how my father, Les, used to watch and encourage me, but my mother, May, also provided great support. She had the hardest job to keep up with all the washing. On most weekends during the season, I played for the school in the morning and would then go straight down to the local park in the afternoon to watch the matches there, as well as having a little kick-around with friends. It was extra practice time and I'd dive around and get dirty and muddy again. On Sunday I would play once more, and so there was a never-ending stream of dirty washing for my mother. She worked in the shop, but had another full-time job keeping my kit clean. That is really appreciated now, although as a youngster you tend to take all this for granted. I used to have a big cooked breakfast on a Saturday morning and go straight out and play, giving no time for digestion. Nowadays, it is realised that it is advisable to have a light meal well before any match.

My representative matches helped me to graduate to a professional career. At the age of ten, I had played for the Leicester Under-11 side. At that time I also played for a spell in the old-fashioned right-half position wearing the number four shirt. When I was 14, I tried playing as centre forward with some success and scored 29 goals in a season of schoolboy soccer. I felt that trying my hand at a number of positions gave me very positive experience, and it also meant that I was covered if I stopped growing.

One interesting game I played in at the age of 14 was for Leicester Boys at the local Saffron Lane stadium. We met

This time I managed to stop the attack, but I was still feeling the effects of flu and Chester-le-Street ran out 3-2 winners.

Chester-le-Street from County Durham in the third round of the English Schools Trophy. David Needham, who went on to play with me in Nottingham Forest's Championship and European Cup-winning side, played in the same team. Colin Todd and Colin Suggett, who both had very successful professional careers, the former winning two Championship medals and 27 caps for England while at Derby, played for Chester-le-Street. It was one of my worst experiences. I had been in bed for a week with a severe bout of flu and got up for the first time two days before the game. I still felt very groggy and had a nightmare of a match. We lost 3-2 and I wish I had spent two more days recovering.

The next big stage in my career was to play for England Schoolboys. It was a great thrill playing in goal for England against Scotland at Wembley in front of 90,000 people. That was a wonderful match for a 15-year-old, especially as we won 3-0. I also played for the Leicester Schoolboys team that reached the final of the English Schools Trophy. We ended up sharing the honours with Swansea after drawing each leg of the final. Both matches ended in a 1-1 draw and I'll never forget a crowd of 20,000 coming along to watch us at Leicester.

Very few people have reached the top of their chosen profession without a little bit of luck along the way. That has certainly applied to my career. I was very fortunate to get into the England Schoolboys side, but made the most of my opportunity. I was picked for a trial at Andover in Hampshire and had a bad game. Afterwards, I was very disappointed and thought I had no chance of making the England team, but I was picked as a reserve for the final trial at Maidstone. It was then that someone else's bad luck gave me my big break. The first-choice goalkeeper didn't turn up because of illness, so I took his place. It is a game I'll always remember. The pitch was covered in snow and I had an absolute blinder. That performance ensured my selection for the England Schoolboys team. Although I believe you make the most of your own luck, that was something that came out of the blue. A little bit of good fortune gave me my first experience of playing in front of a full house at Wembley. It really gave me a taste for more.

My career was helped along by schoolboy soccer, midweek training sessions at Leicester City and the benefits of being in a boys' club. I was part of the original group that founded Blaby Boys' Club. With the help of family, friends and many fund-raising events, we built it up into one of the biggest boys' clubs in Leicestershire. We had a van to take us to a gymnasium in Leicester that we used to hire. Most of the time was spent playing five-a-side in the gym, and two Leicester City professionals used to come along and give us some coaching.

The England Schoolboys squad in Belfast, May 1965.

It was through the Blaby Boys' Club that I gained my first experience of 'international football'. I still remember the excitement when we were told we were going on a trip to Germany, to Hamburg, to play against a local team. When we arrived at the north German city, the first thing I did was to look around all the sports shops to see the different kit they had. The actual game was played on an all-weather pitch. It was a shale surface of a kind I had never seen before, which was a bit rough and abrasive for goalkeeping. But it was great to meet boys of a different nationality and play against them. I would recommend any sports-mad youngster to go abroad with your school or boys' club and play in other countries if ever you get the chance. Players from different nations always have some differences in technique and approach to the game that are interesting to see. It is always important to incorporate other ideas into your game, and there is no better way than by going abroad. Foreign journeys also help young players to mature and experience different food and culture.

Every youngster has players that he idolises and looks up to. They are usually the stars of his local club or the team he supports. It is always awesome to meet the players you admire, especially when they are international footballers. I used to go down to Leicester City on Tuesday and Thursday evenings. A session often ended up with me working out alone with trainer George Dewis. It was he who helped me the most in the early part of my career. His personal tuition gave me great belief in my own ability. We used to go into a little gym at Leicester's Filbert

Street ground and George would put me through my paces, hammering balls at me and forcing me to make saves. Behind the gym was a snooker room and many of the senior players used to spend the afternoon and evening playing a few frames. On leaving, they had to walk through the gym and came past while I was being trained. George would say to the first-team players: 'Come on, see if you can beat this lad.' I recall stars like Gordon Banks, Frank McLintock and Graham Cross trying to hit balls past me. I was diving about on coconut matting in the gym trying to stop their shots. It was a very exciting time for an awe-struck young teenager to compete against the stars, and experiences like that stay in the memory.

I was 15 when I signed for my local team Leicester as an apprentice professional. My development was helped by training with Gordon Banks, and I remember how hard he worked at his game. I watched Gordon and Peter Bonetti in action and admired the great Russian keeper, Lev Yashin – they were the best three goalkeepers around. While trying to learn from the greats, I always felt it was important for me to develop my own style and go my own way in the end. From Gordon I learnt the disciplines of positional play and studied especially how he got into position

Signing up for Leicester City. Watching on are (left to right): Eddie Plumley, my father and manager Matt Gillies.

very early and made goalkeeping look easy. Peter Bonetti's agility caught my imagination and I liked the way he came off his line and caught crosses. Lev Yashin impressed me because he was such a big, athletic man and looked so intimidating. I will always remember how he used to wear all black and created an aura of invincibility before he went onto the pitch.

These were the goalkeepers who inspired me, but, as I worked with Gordon at Leicester, he was the major influence at the start of my career. Gordon went to Stoke when I was 17½ and left me with a permanent place in the Leicester City team. However, I had made my debut at 16½ and I am still the youngest man to play for the club.

I played my first League game in a 3-0 win over Everton, and Fred Pickering, an England centre forward, was playing against me. Three days earlier I had played in a testimonial match at Leicester and enjoyed a good game which made my debut easier. The best possible start for any goalkeeper in his first match is to keep a clean sheet. We reached the FA Cup final in 1969 and I

In flying action for Stoke City, having joined the club for a record fee of £325,000.

I claim the ball during the 0-0 draw against Coventry City which secured Forest their first-ever League Championship in 1977/8.

also collected a Second Division Championship medal with my home town club in 1971.

Stoke City was the next stop. I joined the club for a world record transfer fee for a keeper at the time and had a very successful first season at the Victoria Ground. We were top of the league for a while, but two of our star players got bad injuries and we slipped down to fifth in Division One; at one point we looked as though we might take the Championship. After that promising start, Stoke suffered from financial problems and in my third season with the club we ended up getting relegated. I loved my time with Stoke and had a great rapport with the supporters and local people.

After Stoke I moved on to join soccer's most famous managerial partnership, Brian Clough and Peter Taylor, at Nottingham Forest. It proved to be my most successful spell in club football. I joined in season 1977/8 and we won the First Division Championship. Very few people would have put Forest in the running for the title at the beginning of the season, but we clinched it with a goalless draw at Coventry. I will never forget the match as I made one of my best-ever saves to prevent Coventry striker Mick Ferguson from scoring. That save has been shown on television on many occasions and still gives me great pleasure. Also in that year Forest won the League Cup, but I could not play as I was cup-tied and Chris Woods took my place. The following season, Forest's success continued with two more trophies, the European Cup and another League Cup victory.

To play for Brian Clough and Peter Taylor was a unique experience. Peter Taylor was a wonderful character and, as he was a former goalkeeper himself, we struck up a great relationship. He had a marvellous sense of humour and we also shared a common interest in horse racing – I always enjoyed his company. I also got on well with Brian Clough. There were certain similarities: like me, he was a strong and determined character. I could see a lot of me in both Peter and Brian. That was why I respected them so much and enjoyed playing for them. It was a very successful time at Forest.

When that team broke up after five years, I decided on a change and moved on to Southampton to play for another great manager, Lawrie McMenemy. During my time on the south coast we finished First Division runners-up (Southampton's highest-ever League position) and we reached three semi-finals, two in the FA Cup and one in the League Cup. We were very unfortunate to meet the likes of Liverpool and Everton in the semi-finals. Just before I joined Southampton three famous international stars played for the club – Alan Ball, Kevin Keegan and Mick Channon. I don't know quite what effect I had on them, but Mick Channon left before I played a game, Kevin departed soon afterwards and Alan retired a few weeks later. Lawrie McMenemy's style was a contrast to Brian Clough and Peter Taylor. Lawrie was a great organiser but he did not spend much time on the training pitch. He kept his eye on everything and

At Southampton, Liverpool twice prevented the club from going to Wembley in consecutive seasons, but here I have come off my line quickly enough to stop Ian Rush.

Everton were beaten 3-2 in this game in February 1989, and Derby were well on their way to their best season since 1976.

everybody. Above all, he was an excellent man manager. He delegated well and knew how to talk to players and the club was run on a very professional footing.

I moved back to the Midlands on leaving Southampton to join Derby County. They were enjoying a run of success under manager Arthur Cox and had risen from the Third to the First Division in two seasons. Our first season in the top flight was difficult and we took time to adjust. In our second season, the addition of goalscorer Dean Saunders strengthened the side and we finished fifth in the First Division. However, in our fourth season, 1990/91, Derby were relegated after a season of financial and political problems.

All sportsmen are influenced by older competitors or more experienced players and also by managers, coaches and administrators. In football, senior players and managers can point a youngster in the right direction and develop the correct habits needed to become a successful soccer player. Throughout my career, I have been lucky to come under the guidance of some of the best and most experienced managers in the game. At Leicester City I played for two excellent men in Matt Gillies and

Frank O'Farrell. At Stoke City I worked for the knowledgeable Tony Waddington before joining up with Brian Clough and Peter Taylor at Forest. Even after I had passed the age of 30, Lawrie McMenemy at Southampton and Arthur Cox at Derby still had a big part to play in developing my career.

I was lucky to be educated by a distinguished collection of managers, but that is not what always happens and every aspiring apprentice should consider the club he is joining and the manager and coaches he will be working for. Sound management and good coaching in the formative years could decide whether or not a youngster makes the grade in the highly competitive world of professional soccer. All the advice and encouragement I got from family, coaches and managers helped me to gain a record 125 caps for England. My football education was furthered by over 20 years' experience of international football and top tournaments.

Any youngster playing his first big game feels nervous and a lot of pressure was put on me when I made my debut for England against East Germany in 1970. My old clubmate and mentor, Gordon Banks, had been left out after England's World Cup in Mexico and everyone thought he had been dropped. In fact, Alf Ramsey was trying to find out who was going to be his reserve keeper and decided to pick me and Ray Clemence for the squad. I was given the first chance and had a good game as England beat the Germans 3-1, so establishing myself as Gordon's international deputy.

I had in fact been called over to Mexico the previous year for my first England tour. I had been on an Under-23 team trip and remember arriving back looking forward to a rest. I heard that Gordon Banks had been recalled from the pre-World Cup tournament due to a family bereavement and I was to be his replacement. At the time I just couldn't believe it. The next morning, I flew out to join a squad which included world-famous players like Bobby and Jack Charlton and Bobby Moore. I was a reserve for the first match, when Gordon West played against Mexico, but I was selected to play in Guadalajara against a Mexican XI. It was not a full international, but it was still a valuable introduction to international football. Gordon Banks flew back and played in the last match, against Brazil, and I was a reserve. I remember sitting in the stadium among 200,000 people, watching Pele and other great Brazilian players and thinking what an experience it was for an 18-year-old.

I was in the squad of 28 that went out to Mexico for the World Cup the following year. Sir Alf Ramsey had to cut the squad to 22 and I was disappointed to be one of the six left out. I must impress on any young player with dreams of international football that my career with England had plenty of ups and downs, even

Having been Gordon Banks' understudy at Leicester, I became his deputy at international level after the 1970 World Cup.

though I made a record number of appearances. My worst experience was in 1973 when England failed to qualify for the 1974 World Cup finals. We were knocked out after a draw with Poland, after which Alf Ramsey was sacked. The blame for Poland's goal was levelled at me. Sir Alf was eventually succeeded as England manager by Don Revie, who left me out in favour of my friend Ray Clemence, so I played only two games under his management. Before Revie took over, Joe Mercer had run the side in a caretaker capacity and left me out after a 2-2 draw with Argentina at Wembley. It was a very frustrating time for me to be out of the side for so long.

I came back into the England team when Ron Greenwood took over. He decided to alternate between Ray and me. It was not an ideal situation, but it kept us both on international duty. For the World Cup finals in Spain in 1982, Greenwood decided he would make a final choice and eventually I was picked to be the keeper in the tournament. Reaching the World Cup finals helped to wipe out the memory of the disastrous game against Poland nine years before. The event in Spain was a great experience. We conceded one goal in five matches and were unbeaten when we went out of the tournament. Trevor Brooking and Kevin Keegan were both injured, each making just one brief substitute appearance, and their absence reduced the element of flair in our side.

The next World Cup in Mexico was a great tournament and another landmark in my career. It was very difficult for the north European sides to cope with the heat and the altitude. We tried to acclimatise in similar conditions in Colorado in the United States, where we trained at an air force base. Part of our preparation was a series of strenuous fitness and medical tests. We played in a cauldron in Monterrey, where the pitch was like a Sunday pub team's ground with a bumpy surface and long grass. We lost 1-0 to Portugal, drew 0-0 with Morocco and then played in a rather better stadium and beat Poland 3-0. It was a great match for the two Leicester lads. Gary Lineker scored a hat trick and I kept a clean sheet and made one of the most important saves of my career. In the first minute we were very jittery and a Polish player got through, but I managed a vital stop. Had the ball gone in, the story might have been different.

In the next round of the competition we beat Paraguay 3-0. So far in the competition I had conceded only one goal in four games. In the quarter-finals we met Argentina in that famous match which was decided by Maradona's handball goal. You have to rely on the referee and the linesman in any game of football. The referee may not have been in a good position, but how the linesman did not spot Maradona pushing the ball past me with his hand remains a mystery to this day. The result – Argentina 2, England 1; and so we went out of the tournament.

My first duel with the West Germans in the World Cup finals was back in 1982, when the score finished 0-0. I only just reached this shot which was heading for the top corner.

Shaking hands with Maradona before the quarter-final of the 1986 World Cup. However, it was his left hand which was to do the damage with that infamous 'hand of God' goal.

Big international events usually provide wonderful memories, but the European Championship in Germany in 1988 was a major disappointment. We had a good international record at the time and were rather unlucky to lose our first match of the tournament 1-0 against the Republic of Ireland. Holland were then rather flattered by the scoreline when they beat us 3-1. In our last group game we lost 3-0 to the USSR. By then, the team was out of the competition and the game had no real significance.

However, the England team recovered well from that setback to qualify for the World Cup in Italy in 1990. At the age of 40, I enjoyed the highlight of my career. Nearly every moment of that tournament was sheer delight. I felt I was still playing as well as ever, although I realised Italia '90 would probably be my last big international competition. The Italians certainly know how to put on a show; everything was magnificently staged. The matches were played in superb stadia. We began our group matches in Sardinia, which had a holiday island atmosphere, but any thoughts of relaxation ended after our first match: we drew 1-1 with the Republic of Ireland. The pitch was hard and bumpy and there was a strong wind. I looked at the Republic's team and nearly all their players came from Football League sides. After a first half of non-stop pressure, and with the ball blowing back in my face, it seemed just like a Saturday league match back home and I had to ask myself: is this really the World Cup? It was a very difficult match to play. In our next game, against European Champions Holland, we had to do better. We did improve a little, but failed to score and so had to settle for a goalless draw. Our third game was against Egypt and we needed a point at the very least to qualify for the next stage of the competition. It was 0-0 at half time, but we struck with the only goal of the game in the second half, a Mark Wright header. For me, it was more a feeling of relief than anything else to go through to the next round.

We were up against another European side in the last 16. Belgium were attracting interest as outsiders to win the tournament. They gave us a very close game and I had the kind of luck a goalkeeper needs from time to time when they hit the post twice. There's an old saying for any young player to remember: 'A miss is as good as a mile.' The match looked like a stalemate until David Platt scored in the very last minute of extra time with a superb volley. What was quite encouraging was the fact that we had fought through to the quarter-finals without finding our best form. It is never a bad thing when a team gets good results without playing particularly well.

Preparing for the penalty shoot-out in Turin after the 1-1 draw in the World Cup semi-final against West Germany.

Our opponents in the quarter-finals were Cameroon, the surprise team of the competition. It was another very difficult game. They were strong, physical and very skilful and I had a very busy game. David Platt headed us in front, but Cameroon recovered and took a 2-1 lead. We showed great spirit in fighting back. A penalty from my international room-mate, Gary Lineker, took the tie into extra time. Gary went on to score the winner, also from the spot, to give us a 3-2 victory and a place in the semi-final.

When anyone asks what was the highlight of my international career, I have to say it was that World Cup semi-final in Turin against West Germany. Without doubt we played our best football of the competition and there was very little to choose between the two sides. I remember having to make two decisive saves, but England also went very close to scoring. At the end of extra time, the score was 1-1. As everyone will recall, we went out of the World Cup after a penalty shoot-out, but it was still a memorable match and a wonderful tournament for England. We played another match, losing to Italy in the play-off game to decide third place. It was after that game that I decided to announce my retirement from international football. I had fulfilled nearly all my ambitions and had ended with a record 125 appearances for England. Italia '90 was my third World Cup competition. I had played international football at the age of 40 and had also had the honour of captaining my country.

I always felt that the next logical step in my career was to become a player/manager and was delighted to be given that job at Plymouth Argyle. Although I'm now the oldest professional in the game, I still feel as fit as ever and reckon I could go on playing for a few more seasons yet. When training becomes a chore, I'll hang up the number one jersey and concentrate on being a full-time manager. Although I took over at Plymouth with the club struggling at the foot of the Second Division, I feel there's a lot of potential to be developed. It's a big city and it is quite possible that Plymouth could support a Premier League club.

Several people have asked me if it was a strain taking over a club fighting against relegation in my first spell in management . . . all I can say is that I have enjoyed every moment. As I've mentioned before, in my club and international career I've been lucky to work for some of the greatest managers in the game. They have certainly influenced me, but I'll be implementing my own ideas in running a soccer club.

I owe all these memories to the fact that I learnt my trade thoroughly and received plenty of good advice and guidance along the way. Now I will try to pass some of that experience on to you.

# SHOTS

PREVIOUS PAGE: In training for England.

Shot-stopping is the single most important skill for a goalkeeper to master. The more shots a keeper saves, the more chance his side has of winning a match. A goalie will have to deal with all sorts of shots from many different angles.

# NARROWING THE ANGLE

Perhaps the first discipline a young player needs to learn is how to narrow the angle. That is, how to make shots easier to save by good positional play. It is a question of balancing the distance of a striker from goal with how far you can advance from your line. The idea is to make a forward see as little of the goal as possible, allowing the keeper to make the save much easier than it would have been if he had been rooted on the goal line. In other words, for the forward, the goalkeeper must look a large obstacle and the goal a small target.

Narrowing the angle will depend on the size of the individual goalkeeper. The approach will be slightly different for a goalkeeper of 5 feet 6 inches to that of one who is 6 feet 6 inches. A tall player will be able to come much further off his line than a small one as he won't be so vulnerable to the ball being lobbed over his head. A small goalkeeper should be able to move around goal a little quicker, so if he does not come quite so far, he may be able to get across the goal faster. Goalkeepers therefore have to make individual adjustments as the ability to narrow the angle depends on size and agility.

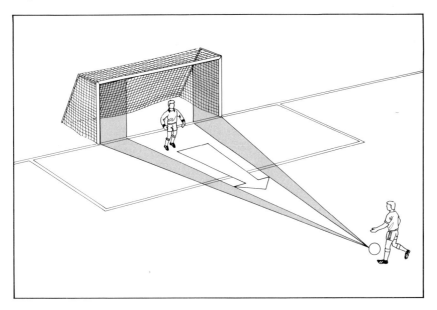

As the keeper comes off his line then the angle available to the striker is clearly narrowed.

Goalkeepers will need to advance further when the striker is coming straight at them as the attacking player will be seeing a bigger target. When shots are hit at an angle, the forward has a smaller area to aim at, so the keeper does not need to advance so far. The further out a shot is struck, the more time there is to see the ball. The goalie has to work out how far to come off the line without the danger of the ball going over him and dipping under the bar.

# TECHNIQUE

In trying to make saves, many goalkeepers use the wrong technique. It is crucial to develop the right habits in stopping shots. Some keepers throw their arms at the ball and their body follows, which means they will not be able to stretch very far to reach the ball. The other mistake made by poor goalkeepers is that they tend to use their feet in the wrong way to make up ground. They cross them over as they go for the ball and lose their balance thus costing split seconds which can so easily lead to a goal. This combination of not using the body to get across to the ball and not using the feet properly means a keeper loses momentum and spring and therefore dives flat. It is rather like two performers on the high board at the swimming baths: the one who masters the movement dives effortlessly with plenty of spring, while the one who gets the technique wrong belly-flops awkwardly into the water making a huge splash.

The correct technique, and our starting point, is to remember that the head and feet are the first things that move to a shot. Try to get the head as far in line with a shot as possible. That will depend, of course, on how fast the ball is travelling. The more you get your head and feet across towards the ball the better. Head and feet move first and the arms are an extension to that. At the end of the movement, the arms come out last to hold the ball or knock it away. It is very important to make sure your body stays compact as you go across the goal to save a shot. Shoulders and head stay slightly forward to give a feeling of compactness and a positive attitude to attacking the ball. Try to get both hands to the ball and, if you are going to catch it, make sure the hands are slightly behind it so you can make the catch and not allow it to slip through your grasp.

I have explained that the feet are important and must not cross over. The best example of how to use feet correctly is to watch a nimble boxer. Try to think of a goalkeeper as being like a boxer in the way he uses his feet and adjusts his body position to keep balanced. The keeper must have his weight in the right position at the right time so he can knock shots away, punch balls or make a catch. A well-balanced body with feet in the right position can make all the difference in goalkeeping. Poor keepers will move across towards the ball using bad footwork and will be awkwardly balanced. Inevitably, they get in a tangle, drop the ball and allow the opposition to score. Just as a boxer with good footwork can take a punch, stay balanced and carry on, so a goalkeeper can hold a hard shot, maintain his balance and start an attacking movement for his team. If you watch a top boxer carefully he will never bring his feet together nor will he cross them over, instead they are always evenly spaced so his weight can go forward or back. For a goalkeeper, it is important to be able to move from side to side very quickly and also to practise moving forwards and backwards when covering the goal area.

Peter Bonetti, the agile and athletic Chelsea and England goalkeeper, dives to make a save.

Always adopt the compact position, with the body dipped slightly forward as part of a positive attitude towards the ball. If a shot comes at you, you should not fall backwards and allow it in. Make sure that you stay supple and loose; the body mustn't be too rigid, but should be like a coiled spring. A keeper must not be so loose and slack that he is unable to react nor must he be so stiff and tight that he cannot move easily. Always remember the three 'S's that sum up a goalkeeper's approach: Springy, Supple and Strong.

Keepers who are very stiff create difficulties for their defenders, because the ball seems to bounce off them like a brick wall, as they have failed to take the pace out of the shot. A goalie should be like a shock absorber. If a shot is hit at you with a lot of pace, you can take the sting out of it if you are supple. Your body will react to the ball. As with a cat leaping off a wall, who absorbs the impact when he lands on the ground because he's supple, lithe and athletic, so it is with goalkeepers. Many have been likened to a cat in their reactions, most notably Peter 'The Cat' Bonetti. Also, when a goalkeeper is very upright he falls backwards when someone hits a shot. Or he may try to move back and then completely lose balance. If he uses the correct technique and bends his shoulders, moves his head forward and is supple, then when he moves into an upright position to take a shot, that is the final position he'll be in to make a save. In this way he reacts again like a coiled spring.

# GETTING YOUR BODY BEHIND THE BALL

The old adage that is applied to so many sports is most important in goalkeeping: 'Get your body behind the ball!' How many times have you heard that shouted out by PE teachers and coaches? To keep up the discipline of getting the body behind the ball, good movement is essential. It will seem rather obvious to suggest that if your head and feet move first towards the ball, then the rest of your body must follow. But that is the best method.

Some coaches will say that you have to catch every ball. I don't completely agree with this, although in principle it is best if you can catch the ball. A keeper who is incorrectly balanced, not using his feet, not getting his body across and not bending at the shoulders will try to catch the ball when he shouldn't, and that's when mistakes are made. If you are going to make a catch don't take chances. If you cannot make the catch, punch or parry the

It is important to get your body behind the ball when making a save, as here when challenged by Brighton's Mickey Thomas.

ball well away with as much power as possible. If the ball's moving with a great deal of pace, fingertips are enough to deflect it away. But when you get across to a shot with both hands, you have to make up your mind whether to catch or parry. A keeper carrying out the correct discipline should be able to get well across his goal and have enough strength and spring to knock the ball away from danger. The important point here is to make up your mind whether to catch, parry away from goal or knock a hard shot away. If you are indecisive you will drop the ball down for scavengers to put it in the net.

Although the body moves across towards the ball, the arms will make the final contact. In many cases, goalkeepers move their body but the ball can go under them as they have not moved their arms quickly enough. Arms go towards the ball once the keeper has made the dive.

# STARTING POSITION

The starting position is where the body should be to react to shots. The feet should be spaced well apart, but no more than the width of the shoulders. Head and shoulders should be slightly bent forward and knees also slightly bent. Hands must be in a comfortable position somewhere around waist height. A goalkeeper needs to vary his body position depending on how far from goal a shot is struck. He needs more of a crouching style for shots from the edge of the box or just inside. The keeper is then in a good position to react to the low shot or one at shoulder height. Beware of the lower ball as a keeper has less time to see the shot. For any higher shots, just a touch will send the ball over the bar. In the crouched position, the keeper's weight will be forward with arms slightly lower to allow time to get the hands down and gain those extra moments to handle the shot.

If you are too upright, shots from around the edge of the box will go past you or underneath you before you have time to move. For shots from a long way out, still bend the shoulders, but remain more upright as you have longer to see the ball. Long shots have further to travel through the air and can dip more, especially at the last moment. The keeper can then react to tip the ball over the bar – hence the need to stay slightly more upright.

The correct starting position to make a save: knees bent, legs apart and weight forward.

The goalie has to be aware of the different types of shots he has to deal with, and the one that skids in front can be the most difficult to keep out. On a hard, uneven pitch it may bounce unsympathetically, while on a wet, soggy surface the ball may skid through. Goalkeepers often fumble the ball because they don't keep their eye on it and their head over it. Sometimes the head goes back and the ball rebounds off a keeper's chest as the ball dips in front of him. So remember to keep your eye on the ball and head down until the very last moment. For the hard, low shot get your head across as far as possible – in that way you have more chance to get behind the ball to make a catch or parry.

# ONE AGAINST ONE

So-called one-against-one situations, when an opposing player breaks clear to challenge the goalkeeper, always provide the most dramatic moments of a match. The keeper has to make up his mind very quickly how he is going to save his side. He has to narrow the angle. If he comes out too quickly, the striker will chip the ball over his head into an empty net. It is vital the goalkeeper judges his rate of advance from goal to the striker. You must be aware that the opposing player may try to chip the ball over you, but more times than not he will attempt to take the goalkeeper on. The chip shot is very difficult even for the most skilful forwards. If you advance too quickly, though, you can make the lob over your head an easier option. You have to make the chip extremely difficult so that only great players will try to score in this way. If they are willing to try – good luck to them!

Once you have eliminated the chance of a chip, stand up and get as close to the striker as possible without rushing too quickly as that can make the striker's mind up. If you move too fast, he can take the ball around you or push it under your body. My secret is that there is a split second when the striker decides that he is not able to put the ball over the goalie's head. If the chip is not on he'll look for a shot. If the player decides not to shoot, you may be able to advance a little quicker. You must remember the important points: keep your footwork and balance right, keep low, stay low and keep your shoulders and head forward. A goalkeeper may be able to make up valuable yards when the opposing player has realised the chip is not possible and decided against a shot. You can then make your advance quicker and crowd him. Once you are two or three yards from the striker, he has to take the ball around you. This is the classic scenario in the one-against-one situation. Stand on your feet, keep low and make

Alan Gowling of Bolton was the loser in this one-against-one confrontation – one of the best saves a keeper can make.

sure he does not get past you. Don't dive or 'lie down' too early, as that will make it too easy for him.

This is a great save to make. If the keeper makes the stop he's a hero. Everyone expects the forward to score. So the pressure is on the attacking player, as the goalie is not expected to make the save. But in these situations I do expect to thwart my opponent. I believe that if the goalkeeper's technique is right, and he does the correct things, he can make it difficult for the forwards. Confidence comes into play. Many keepers panic when strikers run at them, and lose composure when they realise they might give away a goal. They rush out in a hurry and present the opposing player with an easy task. They make up his mind for him and he can take the ball around the keeper or push it under him. The goalkeeper must realise that, by making the save, he can win the game and give his side a boost. There is also a psychological advantage to be won by getting one up on the striker.

Diving at feet is part of a one-against-one situation, but it can also happen in other areas. When a ball breaks in a box, a keeper may have to come off his line and dive in a ruck of feet. On these occasions he may have to throw himself at his own players' feet. Goalkeepers get injuries in these situations by using the wrong technique. It is necessary to show bravery and courage to be in goal, otherwise you are likely to suffer injuries. Some throw their feet at the ball and try to keep their head out of the way and in the process leave it in an upright position. An exposed head can be caught by a knee or foot. This is often the way that serious head injuries are caused.

As you come out, you must get into a low position with knees bent, head and shoulders forward and arms in front of your head. Go low into the ball so your body hits the ground a yard or so behind it. If a striker toe-pokes it just before you get to the ball, it will hit your body anyway. Make sure your line of descent is low so you get your body along the floor before you actually reach the ball. Your head should be shielded, as it is behind your hands and arms as you go in for the ball. Your legs should be well away from the ball.

It is important to remember you cannot go straight at the ball. Go in at an angle so that you can get your body down and across the ball. All keepers will have one side they favour for diving, but it is essential that you can manage to throw yourself to the left or

Diving at players' feet is never easy. Here I have to beat Gary Mabbutt (No 6), Glenn Hoddle and Olaf Thon (No 10) of West Germany to get to the ball.

right. Some goalkeepers come out for the ball and can dive only one way. Try to practise diving in both directions, getting down early and throwing your legs to one side. Try to save balls from every direction and every angle.

# QUICK REACTIONS

Quick reactions are an aspect of goalkeeping that can be misunderstood. I am not simply talking about the reactions necessary for a point-blank save, that glorious moment the crowds love to see. It applies to a far wider range of factors in goalkeeping.

It is most important to look sharp and alert, and then quick reactions can be brought into use in a wide range of instances. Where a keeper's reactions are keen he can read situations as they develop and, for example, cut out the dangerous through ball. A player with sluggish reactions will not have spotted the danger in time. Snooker players see the pockets much bigger when they are cuing the ball well. In soccer it is very similar. When your reactions are quick, you see the ball earlier and so it is much easier to collect. If you pick up the flight of a ball that vital split second earlier, you can react quicker and be more alert and ready for the challenge. If you see a shot from far out a moment earlier, the ball does seem to come at you much slower, with the result that you will make the stop look more comfortable. You will also move your feet and head earlier to gain advantage.

When a shot along the ground takes an awkward bounce or a high ball dips in the air, a keeper with quick reactions will be able to deal with the threat far better. He will keep his head and eye on the ball, see it more clearly, get his body into position and make sure the shot sticks. In this way you can hold on to the ball while a lesser keeper may drop it, and that could be the difference between winning and losing a match.

A boxer in his prime is sharp and alert and trains to quicken his reactions. He can duck, weave and bob to avoid punches. The more he works on these skills, the more he sees the punches coming and avoids them. In the same way, the more reaction work the goalie puts in, the quicker he sees shots coming. A few hundredths of a second in reaction time can determine the difference between an average and a very good keeper. Sharp reactions will give a goalkeeper the chance to stand up much longer. He will quickly see a situation develop and be more confident of stopping his opponent. Good keepers can make a forward miss a chance by looking commanding and formidable.

And that can be down to quick reactions. Without this asset, a goalkeeper will panic, move too soon and 'lie down'. In this case, he will be going for the shot before it has been struck because he has not seen it early enough. It is best to be able to stand up until the last moment to put off the striker. Some goalkeepers will have naturally quick reactions and will think they do not need to work on this aspect of their game. But you always need to keep your reactions finely tuned. If you keep sharp then your game will be sharp.

# HANDLING

The object in dealing with any shot is to make sure you get hands on the ball with your body behind. That, of course, is not always possible. If a shot is high then try to get your head in line. When a shot comes at you at round about chest height, you have to make the decision whether to catch the ball with your hands behind it or take the ball by pulling it into your chest. The technique will be dictated by the pace of the ball. Sometimes, for a hard shot, it is easier to get your palms behind it so, if the ball slips through, your chest will provide a second line of defence and hopefully you can gather any rebound. Any shot coming at waist height will be

Getting your hands behind the ball is crucial to good handling.

difficult to palm. You want to swallow the ball as it comes to you and hug it to you so that it does not slip out of your grasp. When a strike comes in at knee height or bounces in front of you, you can bend your knees and get a leg across the ball. In that way, if you fail to gather it, it will hit your leg or chest. For the low, straight ball you should stoop down and make sure your feet are together. If you miss the ball, it must hit a part of your body. Once again, remember your head must get in line with the ball as quickly as possible.

One last point: it is important that when you get your hands behind the ball, your thumbs should be close together.

# ADVANCING FOR SHOTS

There is a tendency among some goalkeepers to move for the ball as it is being struck. Consequently they are off balance and cannot adjust, so the ball goes under their body or past them. I have developed some exercises (*see* page 50-55) to help keepers come forward and get into position early. In narrowing the angle, you need to get off the goal line and into position before your opponent hits the ball. Try to read the situation and anticipate when someone is about to shoot, remembering what I have

There's no way through for Steve Archibald of Spurs in this game against Nottingham Forest.

already mentioned about using good footwork and taking up the crouched positions. It is vital to be poised in order to carry out the orthodox manoeuvre of being able to get your legs out of the way and your body, head and arms down to the ball. You may notice that when some keepers move out too quickly, their feet shoot out first and they cannot stop their momentum. When goalies block a lot of balls with their feet, it is often because their body is not in the right position. Sometimes you may be able to block the ball only with your feet, especially with hard, low shots. It is important to remember, though, that if you stop the ball with your legs and feet, that will create rebounds and give the attackers a chance to score.

Shots which streak through close to a keeper's body are the ones he has the greatest problems with when he is advancing. Most goalkeepers can get their hands to shots when the ball is going away from the body and they are stretching to dive. However, it is possible to make good saves close to the body if you advance at the right time and get your body into position early for the shot.

When narrowing the angle, some keepers start by advancing from the goal line. This is the wrong approach, as you will run off the line too quickly and not get into position early. Instead, start from slightly further out. As we discussed, in narrowing the angle you have to be far enough off the line to get into position and stand up, but not so far that an opponent can chip the ball over your head. Remember, if you stand rooted to the line, there's not much chance of stopping a shot in the corner. If you advance a little the striker has less to aim at.

Good goalkeeping techniques can gain those valuable split seconds that make all the difference between making a stop and letting in a goal. Some keepers think their style is fine and is appropriate to their build and agility; they can point to many good saves. But just think how much better they would be if they gave themselves more time to save shots and they improved their technique. However successful you are, you must always be prepared to develop your technique.

# SHOOTING GALLERY

In this exercise, the keeper faces a salvo of shots from different angles. This is a good routine to help positional play and narrowing the angle. All you need is a full-size goal, four strikers and plenty of footballs.

**A** The keeper stands in his goal facing four strikers, who are lined up round the edge of the D.

**B** The striker on the left-hand corner of the D has the first shot.

**C** The goalie gets down quickly to make a save.

**D** As the keeper gets in position, the striker on the right-hand corner of the D lets fly. Note that I have come out to the edge of the six-yard box to narrow the angle.

*(continued overleaf)*

**E**  The goalkeeper goes down to make a save at the last moment.

**F**  After the save, another striker shoots. They can vary the exercise by occasionally trying the chip shot.

# SHOOTING STAR

Shooting Star is a competitive exercise between a keeper and a striker. This is a good discipline for working on narrowing the angle. The game is played in a full-size goal. All you need is a friend, a cone and a football.

**A**  A cone is placed at an angle to the goal just inside the penalty area. A striker stands three yards behind the cone, while the keeper stands alert just off his line.

**B**  The striker runs up and dummies to the right or left of the cone, pretending it is a defender.

**C** The striker hammers in a shot.

**D** The keeper, having advanced and narrowed the angle, makes a save.

**E** The striker must vary the way he veers around the cones, which gives him good practice at shooting with either foot.

**F** Sometimes shots will be hit high. Move the position of the cone to vary the angle of approach. As the goalkeeper's confidence and skill improves, the cone can be brought closer.

# STAND AND DELIVER

This is called Stand and Deliver as the keeper has to run forward, stand up and take a variety of deliveries. This exercise is good for improving footwork and gives practice at narrowing the angle. All you need is a goal five to six yards wide marked by cones, a server and a few footballs. Try to repeat the routine ten times.

**A** The keeper gets ready in a crouched position a few yards back between the cones. The server stands facing him about 12 yards away from the goal line.

**B** As soon as the keeper advances, using small, quick steps, the striker begins to run up to the ball. Note how my weight and head are well forward as I move.

**C** The striker hits the ball just before the goalie reaches his line.

**D** The server should vary his shots.

**E** The goalkeeper saves the ball and returns it for the exercise to start again. The keeper relaxes between each save.

# OBSTACLE COURSE

This is the same routine as Stand and Deliver, but with added obstacles specially designed to improve footwork. For this exercise you will need a few more footballs, but otherwise the set-up is exactly the same. Try to repeat ten times.

**A** This is the same set-up as for Stand and Deliver, except the goalie is faced with three to six balls spaced two feet apart between him and the goal line.

**B** The keeper runs over the balls using short, quick steps.

*(continued overleaf)*

**C**  As he is clearing the last ball the server volleys or half-volleys a shot at him. Good balance is vital for the goalkeeper.

**D**  The keeper has to get into position quickly to react to the shot. He then relaxes and the routine is repeated.

# SIDE STEP

This is another variation on Stand and Deliver. Some markers are needed.

**A**  Three to six markers are arranged in a zig-zag pattern between the keeper and the goal line.

**B**  The keeper advances forward using small steps (remembering not to bring the feet together), running to touch each marker.

**C**  Just as the goalie touches the last marker, the server can fire shots at him.

# THE RUBBER BALL ROUTINE

We call this The Rubber Ball Routine because the keeper has to be up and down very quickly, bouncing like a ball to ensure that he stops each shot as it comes in. To speed things along, use one ball only, as this exercise is designed to help improve fitness, agility and reactions. Try to keep going for 10 shots or so at a time, and then increase the routine to 20. All you need for this exercise are two cones or soft markers (to avoid injury) five yards apart for the goal, a ball and two friends.

**A**  The three players are positioned in a triangular formation. A server stands next to one of the cones and throws the ball to a kicker six yards away in front of the goal. Note how I am standing: head and shoulders forward, knees bent to ensure the quickest reactions.

**B**  The kicker volleys the ball at the keeper. He should vary his shots, aiming high, low or short to keep the goalie guessing.

*(continued overleaf)*

**C**  The keeper makes the save.

**D**  He then throws the ball straight back to the server and gets up as quickly as possible . . .

**E**  . . . ready to take the next shot. The server and kicker must not wait for the goalkeeper to be properly positioned, so he is always in motion.

# THE TWIST

This exercise is called The Twist as the keeper has to spin quickly to save the ball. It's a routine that will speed up your reactions. All you need is a server, a few footballs and a goal five to six yards wide marked out by cones. Repeat it about a dozen times.

**A** The keeper stands with his back to the server, with his feet slightly apart in the typical crouched position, ready to take the ball.

**B** The server shouts 'Turn!' the moment he strikes the ball. The goalkeeper has to spin from the hips and face the shot.

**C** The keeper must use his feet quickly to get into position to make a save.

**D** He then throws it back to the server to repeat the exercise. The server must vary his delivery to keep the goalie guessing.

# THE ROCKING CHAIR

This is a good routine for shot-stopping, agility and fitness, and one in which the keeper has to learn how to rock himself back onto his feet. All you need to perform the exercise is a server and a few footballs. Try to carry out eight saves to the right and eight to the left.

**A**  The server throws the ball a yard or two to the goalie's right.

**B**  The keeper dives . . .

**C**  . . . and makes the save.

**D**  After making the save he throws the ball back to the server while still on the ground.

**E** After returning the ball the keeper has to bounce up. He should use his shoulders and the side of legs in a rocking motion to get up quickly. (Try to avoid using arms and knees to get off the floor.)

**F** The server then repeats the throw, moving the keeper along to the right. After eight throws he moves back along to the left to finish roughly where he started.

# ONE AGAINST ONE

One Against One is another competitive routine, with the keeper pitting his wits against a striker running at him. This is good practice for narrowing the angle and diving at a forward's feet. The exercise is carried out on a full-size pitch.

**A** The goalkeeper stands ready on the edge of the six-yard box. A striker stands with a ball at his feet on the edge of the D.

**B** The striker comes forward to try to score . . .

*(continued overleaf)*

**C** . . . while the keeper gets ready to save the shot or the chip and begins to advance to narrow the angle.

**D** The striker, deciding against the shot or the chip, moves into the box. The keeper begins to advance and gives the attacker a difficult choice as to whether to place the ball or dribble around him.

**E** Once the striker is committed, the goalie tries to crowd him and force him to try to dribble past.

**F** The keeper is then ready to pounce at the striker's feet.

**G** He goes in with hands outstretched . . .

**H** . . . and gathers in the ball. Note that my head is well out of the way.

# DIVE BOMB

This is an exercise for practising diving at forwards' feet. It is a good method for improving your technique in one of the more difficult aspects of goalkeeping. All you need is a marker, a server and a few footballs. Try to do ten dives at a time.

**A** The keeper stands by his marker, with the server about 12 yards away.

**B** The server rolls the ball about six yards to the goalie's right, left or straight at him.

**C** Note that when I dive forward I keep my head well behind my hands and my feet out of the way. This is the safest technique.

**D** The goalkeeper must learn to be able to dive straight forward as well as both left and right. You must really explode forward to take the ball. The keeper then returns to the starting position.

# CROSSES

Dealing with crosses or centres is a discipline that many goalkeepers fail to master, even at the highest level. It is surprising that keepers who are super shot-stoppers can be inept when it comes to crosses. The problem often goes back to a player's beginnings in schoolboy and junior football. At an early age, goalies tend to concentrate on shot-stopping and making spectacular saves. One of the difficulties for goalkeepers is that few youngsters have the strength and accuracy to put over the centres needed to test them.

Catching crosses is probably the second most important part of goalkeeping after shot-stopping. A keeper who is weak on crosses will always have a problem with his game and his confidence will be affected. In local or parks soccer you will often see a goalkeeper make three good saves, then come out for a cross, completely misjudge it and give away a goal. At moments like this, the good saves and stops are forgotten, the goalie loses confidence, the defence becomes jittery and problems develop.

The simple and obvious fact about taking crosses is that the keeper has the advantage over his opponents that he is able to use his arms and hands. He should be able to get above their heads to catch or punch the ball. He can prevent menacing balls into the box from developing into an even more dangerous situation. One of the best sights in soccer is to see a goalkeeper come off his line and catch the ball cleanly – all danger evaporates and defenders look relieved. When a defence is weak in the air and has no good headers of the ball, a goalie can make up for the deficiency. If a keeper is confident when dealing with crosses and teams make sure they defend well in other areas, then they will not be caught out by a high ball into the box. The ball crossed in close to the goal must always be the keeper's.

PREVIOUS PAGE: Knowing how to deal with crosses is a vital part of the goalie's art.

ABOVE: The danger from this Italian corner kick in 1973 is cut out. This was also Bobby Moore's last game for England, but it was not until June 1989 that I overhauled his record number of caps. (*Colorsport*)

RIGHT: Italy were the opponents again for my last match for England – at the end of Italia '90 when we won medals for coming fourth. (*Mark Leech*)

PREVIOUS PAGE: At full stretch to deny West Brom during my Nottingham Forest days. (*Colorsport*)

In training for England.   (*Action Images*)

ABOVE: Diving at the feet of Spurs striker Garth Crooks.   (*Colorsport*)

BELOW: Practising the same move in training (*see* page 59-60) helps a keeper to be confident to deal with the situation when it arises in a match.   (*Colorsport*)

ABOVE: Tipping the ball beyond the reach of Altobelli of Italy. (*Bob Thomas Sports Photography*)

RIGHT: Bert Millichip presents me with an award for becoming the world's most-capped player at the game against Holland in the 1990 World Cup. (*Empics*)

ABOVE: There is no way through for Ray Houghton this time in the 1988 European Championships. (*Colorsport*)

LEFT: Pat Jennings and I shake hands after England's 1-0 triumph over Northern Ireland in the February 1985 World Cup qualifier. Both of us would go on to play in Mexico in 1986. (*Bob Thomas Sports Photography*)

ABOVE: Punching clear for Nottingham Forest against local rivals Derby County. (*Colorsport*)

BELOW: Cameroon striker Onam Biyick was just one of their players to make a huge impression during the 1990 World Cup. (*Empics*)

Reaching out across a crowd of players I can punch clear and so help England on to a 1-0 victory in 1988 over our oldest rivals, Scotland. (*Bob Thomas Sports Photography*)

# CATCHING THE BALL AT THE HIGHEST POINT

The fundamental point in taking crosses is to catch the ball at the highest point. In other words, the keeper has to take the ball as he leaps furthest from the ground with his arms fully stretched. It is a mistake to wait for the ball to drop when it comes into the area. A keeper should not be taking the ball while rising or on the way down. Some youngsters wait for the ball to drop onto their chest or make a catch with their arms bent, because they are not confident of reaching the centre or they do not have the judgement to take the ball early. If a goalkeeper waits for the ball to drop, problems will arise because attackers can get in front of him and beat him to the ball. He will have lost the big advantage of being able to use his hands.

Several factors are combined in catching at the highest point. It is important to get your arms up early to take the ball. In the starting position, the arms have to be held relatively high; do not bring your arms up from the side of your body as you will lose a crucial split second in going for a centre. Challenging forwards will make life very difficult if you don't get your arms up early enough to catch the ball. A high starting position will ensure you get your arms above attacking players.

By catching the ball at the highest point, this Dutch attack in the 1990 World Cup finals was prevented from becoming a danger to English hopes of proceeding in the competition.

When going for centres, your head must be in line with the incoming ball and behind it. Although it is not always possible, you need to get your head as near to the ball as you can when going for a cross. As with shot-stopping, it is essential to get your feet into position early to take the ball at the highest point. You must also remember to use small strides so you can adjust the position of your feet quickly. This will help you retain your balance and enable you to react swiftly to move forwards, backwards or sideways. If your feet are well balanced then you'll get good spring and be able to get those arms up early to make the catch.

Once you've got into position, it is essential to get your hands behind the ball. If you come out for a cross on a wet and windy day, you want to make sure the ball 'sticks' in your hands. When someone makes a challenge, you have to be able to hold on to the ball despite being barged and bumped. The right approach is to keep your eyes on the ball as you take the cross. Then complete the movement with a safe catch with your hands wrapped around the ball.

Taking a cross at the back post for Forest against one of my former clubs, Leicester. The momentum has carried the ball behind my head, but this is as it should be when catching at the highest point.

When you catch at the highest point it may appear as though you are actually taking the ball over the back of your head. This is because you will be reaching the ball at full stretch but the momentum of the ball can force your hands backwards. That creates the impression that you have caught the ball behind you. When a goalie takes the ball too low, his finishing point will be directly above his head. So don't be put off if you appear to be going backwards when you make a catch.

It is important to realise that when you go for a centre you cannot always make the perfect catch. Some keepers tend to rush at the ball with long strides and jump into the cross. This is not the best way to take the ball consistently and safely. There will always be the chance of an error if you do not use your feet correctly. Last-minute adjustments will lead to clumsy movements, poor balance and a likelihood that you will fail to catch a cross properly and this will put the pressure back on your defenders. If you take three or four big strides and try to make a catch, you may get underneath the ball, particularly if the wind takes it away from you. The correct manoeuvre is to get into position early using short steps, watch the cross carefully and jump into the cross at the last moment. If your balance is good and your arms are in a high starting position you should be able to cut out any silly mistakes and minimise the chance of spilling the ball.

Taller players will have an obvious advantage when taking crosses, but quite often I've seen goalkeepers waste those extra inches because they lack agility or they do not use their feet quickly enough. Also, big keepers may be prone to using large steps, as a result they'll lose spring and the advantage of their height.

If you are small, it does not mean you are likely to have a weakness when dealing with crosses – you may have an advantage in agility over a bigger person. Smaller keepers may have to learn to jump and spring a little more, use their feet quicker and perhaps punch more than a taller player. Punching can sometimes be a very positive option, rather than a last resort when combatting crosses. If you punch a ball 20 yards or so clear of the penalty box, the immediate danger is cleared and it gives your team a chance to regain possession. By punching more crosses clear, a smaller goalie will have another advantage. He can make his mind up to attack at the earliest possible moment and get in front of attacking players. With natural agility, timing and deft footwork a small keeper can be very effective at cutting out centres.

# PUNCHING

Although we have shown that there are advantages to fisting the ball clear, particularly for small keepers, punching is generally looked on a last resort. Without wishing to create confusion, I would say that usually it is far better to catch than punch, but if you can punch well that might be an advantage in certain situations. Many keepers try to make a desperate catch under pressure in a ruck of players when a punch would be safer and simpler. Always remember that goalkeepers are judged more on their mistakes than their saves. If you come out and punch the ball 20 yards, that is not the worst action to take and it does not mean you are a poor keeper. By catching the ball you snuff out any threat, but a good punch clear is a better bet than fumbling and dropping the ball and giving away a goal.

Punching is an art; if you master the action it will give you a big advantage. Goalies who cannot punch get flustered and try to catch balls when they should not. When a keeper isn't able to decide whether to catch or punch, he gets caught in two minds, makes mistakes and loses confidence.

The punching action is a simple straight jab, rather in the style of a classical boxer. If your arms are up early in position your fist should need to travel only for a short distance. The punching action should be as straight as possible rather than a hook or an

Sometimes punching is the safest option, as here where the Cologne striker has got up well to make my job more difficult. The Forest defence was able to regroup and so ensure a 1-0 victory to take us through to the European Cup final of 1979.

uppercut (*see* page 80-81). Try to make sure you get a firm contact on the ball. The wrong technique is used by keepers who take an extravagant swing at the ball, often bringing their arms up from their side. The shorter and straighter you make your jab for the ball, the more chance you have of hitting the target. If you take a wild swing, you've little chance of making a firm contact and clearing the ball from the danger area.

It is always more helpful to your defence to punch high. If you fist out the ball at head height or below, an opposition player can head or chest it down and set up a scoring chance. But, if you fist the ball high in the air, defenders will have more time to get underneath the ball and block any danger. Practice is vital to make sure you get the necessary distance when you punch out.

The double-fisted punch is another weapon in the keeper's armoury. This can be employed to gain maximum power. Principally, it is used when balls are coming straight at you and not played in from the wing. It is a useful tactic as quite often you can get both arms above attacking players and really thump the ball clear. Another advantage of the double-fisted punch is that it gives you a wider area of contact on the ball and therefore greater accuracy when making a clearance.

# POSITIONING

A goalkeeper's positioning has to be correct when dealing with crosses. Some goalies tend to be frozen on their line. Others go to the near post to cover centres and have to move backwards to deal with any balls delivered beyond them. Once going backwards for crosses the keeper is at a disadvantage. It is difficult to move quickly and you cannot see what's happening behind you unless you've got eyes in the back of your head. The secret is to minimise the distance you have to go backwards. It is better to go forwards and sideways, as you have better vision and more awareness of what is going on and it is also much more tricky to catch when moving backwards. The aim of your positional play should be to give you the best possible chance to cover all areas in and around the goal when centres are coming over from every possible distance and direction.

If a cross is coming from a short distance, you need to be closer to the near post. When the ball is played in from a longer distance, the best position to take up is nearer to the far post. The reason is very simple, when a ball is crossed from a closer point and the goalkeeper is at the far post he will not have enough time to move forward and guard the huge area of goal in front of him.

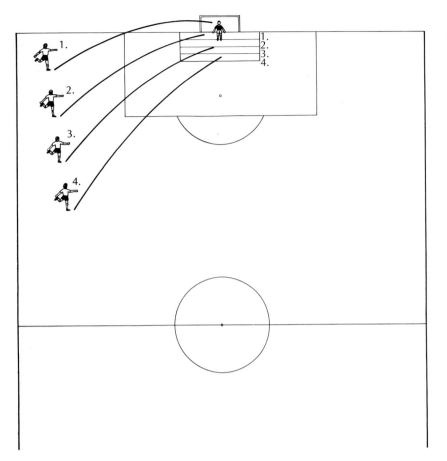

When the cross comes from the by-line (position 1), the goalie must be close to his line (position 1). The deeper the cross the further out he can come.

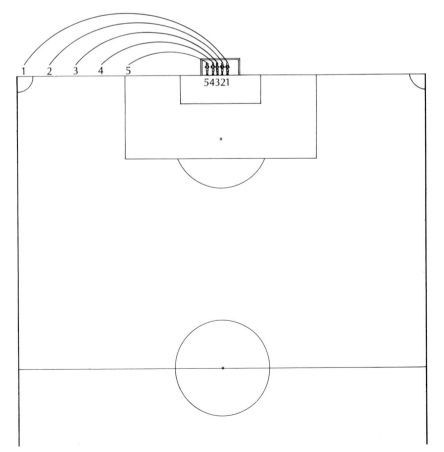

If an attacker has reached the by-line, the nearer he is to the goal (position 5) the closer the keeper should be to the near post (position 5) as he would not be able to cover that area from position 1.

When a ball is delivered from a greater distance, he will have time to cover the far post and move forward to meet any danger. When balls come from either the by-line or deeper positions, it is important for a keeper to advance a little off his line. It is a question of judgement that will improve with experience and practice. You must make sure your near post is covered but give yourself as much chance as possible to get to the far post without leaving the near one open.

Make up your mind as early as possible about what you are going to do to combat a cross. You might opt to get in front of a forward and punch clear or go for a clean catch. Do not delay your decision until the last moment – the biggest errors are made when the keeper is making up his mind as he is about to take a cross.

Assessing the flight of a ball can be very difficult. Centres can be hit with pace or gently lobbed, they may swerve, loop or appear to hang in the air. Once again, essential principles apply. Keep your feet well balanced, assess the type of ball and decide on your approach to the problems presented as quickly as possible. Remember that on very windy days, centres can either get held up in the air or be carried away by a gust. If a cross is dropping short, attack the ball and make sure you get both hands to it for a safe catch. Moving fast towards the ball creates more impact, so be careful not to let it slip through your hands.

Quick decision-making can help you to outwit an opponent. You may get in front of him to catch or punch clear, or you can stay behind him if he jumps too early for the ball. You may jump with an attacker and punch the ball away from his head. In situations when you have to go backwards, try to catch the ball in front of your head in order to stay on your feet.

The correct 'take off' position will help a keeper to gain maximum height when jumping for a cross. Try to take off on one leg and use your other knee and arms to haul you up. This should help your leap. If you use a two footed jump, you'll need to use thighs and arms to get maximum lift, but it is best to use this approach only with the high, looping ball.

Goalkeepers should get the best possible vision of a cross coming in. Wait for the moment a ball is kicked before you assess its flight. Don't rush off your line anticipating where the ball is going to go. The line of the cross and the pace of the ball will determine how you move out. Once again, continuous practice is essential. When you are at full stretch and suddenly find you cannot catch or punch because the ball is caught by the wind, all you can do is deflect it away. That can still be very effective. If you just get a touch and help the ball on its way, that can take it off the heads of opponents or push it over the bar.

# MANOEUVRES

When going backwards, especially towards the far post, some keepers move with their body square to the ball. That will restrict movement. When going backwards it is better to turn sideways so you can go left or right, depending on which way you want to jump. Some goalies go backwards so clumsily they lose balance and fall over.

When moving to take a cross, it is important that defenders know what the goalkeeper is going to do. Try to shout or give an indication of your intentions. In most cases, it is better when a keeper calls for the cross and claims it. If there is no time to shout and defenders get in the way, then that's just too bad. Otherwise you must make short, sharp calls. When you want defenders to clear the ball, it is best to shout, 'away'. When you come off your line to make a catch or punch then bawl out, 'keeper's ball' or 'keeper's'.

# CHALLENGES

A goalkeeper comes under great pressure when he is challenged at crosses, particularly by tall players. If an opponent is close, try to make sure you have some space to jump into and that you will not be impeded. In a crowded goalmouth you must be able to stand your ground when an opposing player takes up a position by you. You can get leverage by standing alongside someone, also try to manoeuvre yourself around him by using your body weight. It is important to be the boss and dictate to the opposition. You should be able to stand your ground shoulder to shoulder with powerful players and still manage to catch or punch the ball. Forwards often rush in with little chance to make contact and try to put you off. Don't be intimidated, concentrate on reading the cross, judge the situation on its merits and keep your eye on the ball.

When crosses are played in to the near post, you will foil forwards by taking the ball at the earliest possible point. Try to move forward to the ball, rather than diving out to meet it. If keepers take the ball before it reaches the near post, then forwards will have little chance of sneaking in front of them. Take the ball at the earliest opportunity but do not overstretch and drop it. Sometimes on crosses you will realise that the ball is going to bounce in front of you. Some keepers make the fatal mistake of waiting for the bounce before trying to gather the ball.

By moving forward to deal with a cross to the near post, I have denied Alex McLeish of Scotland a scoring opportunity.

They fear that if they attempt to take the ball early they will fumble it. It is better to attack the ball and scoop it up on the bounce to stop forwards nipping in .

I mentioned that it is always better to catch a cross, but when you are being challenged for a centre that is dropping on or near the bar, safety first is the best policy. In this situation don't punch, but palm the ball over the bar and so help to cut out any possible error.

Combatting centres and crosses is the most difficult part of goalkeeping. Crosses can be lobbed high, hit at head height or driven low. The ball can swerve, dip or be blown by the wind. A keeper can be impeded by opposition players and his own defenders at times. The only way to sharpen your skills is to deal with a barrage of crosses in training.

# JACK IN THE BOX

In this routine a goalkeeper imitates a Jack in the Box by the way he springs up and down. This is an exercise carried out in a full-size goal with the help of a server and a few footballs. It's a good work-out for helping footwork, fitness, agility and catching the ball at the highest point. Repeat this about eight times as quickly as possible.

**A** The keeper touches a ball placed on the line. A server stands on the byline between the six-yard and 18-yard line.

**B** The moment the keeper touches the ball on the line, the server throws the ball in high with an underarm action.

**C** The keeper must use plenty of spring to attack the ball and catch it.

**D** As soon as he's caught the ball he must repeat the exercise.

**E**  When the keeper touches the ball on the line the server throws in again. He can vary his throws by hurling them high to all parts of the six-yard box and delivering the occasional one at waist height.

**F**  Sometimes the routine can be varied and the keeper can punch the ball instead.

# ME AND MY SHADOW

In this routine another player sticks close to the keeper to try to impede him. This is a good way to help a goalie decide whether to catch or punch. It also gives him confidence to hold his position under pressure. The exercise takes place in a full-size goal area with a server and one other player. Practise for a few minutes.

**A**  The keeper stands alongside an attacking player in the goalmouth.

**B**  The player tries to get in the goalie's way and jostle him, but the keeper must stand his ground.

**C**  A server crosses the ball in from different angles. The goalkeeper must get his arms up early, or else it might be difficult to do so as the ball arrives.

*(continued overleaf)*

**D** The keeper takes the ball at the highest point, giving the attacker no chance.

**E** The goalie may opt to punch the ball away if a catch is dangerous.

# LOOK BEFORE YOU LEAP

In Look Before You Leap, the keeper has to use good judgement when coming out to catch the ball. This is great practice for timing an advance off the line. It's also a useful exercise for working on springing into the ball and for punching as well. You'll need a full-size goal, a server and another player.

**A** A server plays the ball in from the corner of the penalty area. The keeper gets ready to take the ball. Another player stands just in front of the penalty spot ready to attack.

**B** The keeper has to make up ground quickly, using small steps and ensuring he does not arrive too early.

**C** The attacker must try to get a head to the ball if possible.

**D** The keeper springs to take the ball at the highest point. The server should aim anywhere between the six-yard box and the penalty spot, sometimes hitting in lower crosses.

# SHUTTLE LAUNCH

In this exercise the keeper has to move from side to side continuously and jump high for the ball. This helps to build up the thigh muscles and develop spring. The goalie will also improve his footwork, making himself as balanced and nimble as a boxer. Carry out the routine in a full-size goal with the help of two servers and a couple of footballs. Try to do six leaps to either side.

**A** The keeper stands in the centre of his goal, just off the line. Two servers are placed facing a post just outside the six-yard line.

**B** One server lobs the ball underarm higher than the crossbar, the keeper has to move across and leap to take the ball just inside the post.

*(continued overleaf)*

**C** The keeper throws the ball back and then moves across to the other side of the goal to catch the other ball. It is important to use short, quick steps when going sideways, without crossing them over or bringing them together.

**D** Then the second server lobs a high ball to the other post, having waited for the keeper to get back to the centre of the goal again before he throws the ball. Remember: good footwork and a high leap are essential.

# SALMON LEAP

This is called the Salmon Leap as it really makes a goalie jump high for the ball. It's an exercise that's useful for fitness, footwork and stamina. It's also good practice for dealing with chips and going backwards for crosses. You need a full-size goal, a few footballs and a server to help you. Carry this out as a continuous shuttle exercise, repeating the movement eight times.

**A** The keeper stands on his line with a ball in front of him at the edge of the six-yard box. The server stands just in front of the penalty spot and has a number of footballs ready to throw.

**B** The keeper comes out and bends to touch the ball on the six-yard line.

**C** As soon as he's touched the ball, that's the signal for the server to hurl a ball high over the keeper's head, aiming for it to drop just under the crossbar.

**D** The keeper moves back quickly to leap and catch the ball or tip it over the bar. (Remember to turn to the side when moving backwards. If the ball is going to the right, turn to the right and vice versa).

**E** As soon as the keeper has made the save he has to touch the ball on the six-yard line to repeat the movement. Note that I am well balanced and looking up all the time.

**F** The server should vary his throws to the keeper's right and left and straight over his head to make it as hard as possible for him.

# UP THE WALL 1

**A** Stand facing a gym wall.

**B** Hurl the ball hard against the wall.

**C** Leap to punch the rebound away one-handed.
Remember to use a short jab only.

# UP THE WALL 2

**A** Use the corner of the gym for punching practice. Throw the ball against the wall.

**B** Punch the ball either against the adjacent wall to one side . . .

**C** . . . or in the opposite direction.

**D** Leap to reach balls thrown high against the wall.

**E** Practise two-fisted punches, making sure to get a firm contact. In this way you can get maximum height and distance.

**F** This is how you should punch a ball. Aim to hit through the centre.

# QUALITIES

A thorough knowledge of strategy and a high degree of technical expertise do not necessarily produce a top-class keeper. In the previous chapters I have hinted at other qualities that are needed for the number one job in football. But there are six vital ingredients that help to make a good goalkeeper.

PREVIOUS PAGE: My first day as player/manager at Plymouth Argyle.

# 1 SIZE

There is no doubt that height and strength are an advantage for a keeper, but their importance can be overstated. People assume that you have to be built like Goliath to play between the posts, but that's not strictly true. At the professional level, goalkeepers tend to be 6 foot or more, but there have been plenty of exceptions to the rule: in the First Division this season, both Steve Cherry of Notts County and Hans Segers of Wimbledon were under 6 foot. Many youngsters tend to feel they cannot go in goal because they are too small. But you can be of any size to play in goal.

Size is important when it comes to balls being chipped over the head and also when coming out for crosses. If you are taller, you will have more reach to enable you to get to certain shots. This is not always the case as other factors have to come into the reckoning. It is no use being tall and strong without having other qualities to complement your size, like agility. A smaller person may overcome his lack of stature because he has mastered the other crafts of goalkeeping where height and weight don't count so much. As we mentioned in the previous chapter, smaller keepers may not have a disadvantage when dealing with crosses. They may be quicker at getting to the ball and be just as effective by punching the ball away more.

Yes, height and strength are an advantage but that should not discourage smaller players from taking up goalkeeping.

# 2 AGILITY

When people talk about agility, they think of Olympic gymnasts who can produce extraordinary springs and somersaults. A goalkeeper doesn't need these sort of movements, but he does need to be supple and elastic. There's an expression that a keeper

Agility is a crucial part of a goalie's repertoire of skills.

must be like a rubber ball. He has to bounce up and down and around the goalmouth. This is where his agility really counts. As a youngster I used to train at Leicester City on two evenings a week. Most of my work was carried out in a goal six yards wide. I used to stand up and bounce the ball out to the coach who would volley and half-volley the ball back to me. He used to drive the ball low and the routine was carried out with just one touch all the time. As soon as I had saved the shot, I had to throw the ball back. I was up and down like a yo-yo springing high and diving low (*see* page 99-100). My agility improved no end and so did my fitness.

Agility is a quality some people are born with, while others find it difficult to acquire. As with many aspects of goalkeeping, the more practice you have the better you will be. The exercise I have talked about at Leicester was quite basic but, as I worked at it, I could see the improvement in my game. I was always fairly agile, but these sessions improved that part of my game even more.

There are things you can do if you are not naturally agile that will improve your technique. For example, when you dive to save a shot, there is a method of rolling up off the ground using your shoulders and legs to bounce straight back up, instead of using your hands and knees. There are also ways of turning your body and bending your knees in the right direction to give you the best body position to spring from. There is also the point I made about getting your footwork right by using short steps instead of long strides to help you to keep balanced. Using the right technique can improve your agility and there are plenty of exercises you can practise so that even the stiffest and clumsiest mover can improve his goalkeeping.

The point I am making is that it is very important to become as agile as possible. In a match situation, agility is probably the single quality the goalkeeper needs most. Without agility you will not be able to bring off the incredible saves that the crowd wants to see and that distinguish a very good goalkeeper from the average. There is nothing better than to see a keeper fly across goal and fingertip the ball away or catch it with a tremendous spring. It is also exciting to see a goalkeeper come off his line, catch the ball at the highest point and fall on the ground because he stretched so far for the ball. When a cross is driven in and a goalie dives out at head height and makes a catch among a group of rampaging forwards, this is another great moment for the keeper and the crowds. Goalkeepers can also bring the fans to their feet by coming off their line quickly to dive at a player's feet. All these saves would be made more difficult without a great deal of agility on the keeper's part.

# 3 CONCENTRATION

As in any sport, the mental side of football is becoming more and more important. It is no use having great ability in carrying out your work if your concentration is not right: your game will fall apart, you will make silly mistakes and look a bad or average player. I cannot stress how important it is to keep your concentration during a game. That is much more difficult for a goalkeeper than for an outfield player. Sometimes you may have a great deal of work to do and be saving shots all the time. That will mean you are constantly involved in the game and your mind will be fully occupied. There are other times when you won't have a save to make and you will have to concentrate on what I call

Concentration is vital for a goalkeeper at any level, especially as here, in the 1986 World Cup finals, when any lapse could destroy the hopes of the nation.

'bread-and-butter goalkeeping'. That is when you have to catch the odd cross or field a through ball, but you do not have to stop any direct shots. In the last minute you may have to make one vital save and still be concentrating enough to make sure you are sharp and alert for that moment.

In a sport like snooker, a player can perform exceptionally well for several frames and then make a silly mistake and let someone in and never regain control of the match. In cricket, a batsman makes an error through a lapse in concentration and he is out. In any game you must be competing all the time. Your mental attitude is vital. You must not become lethargic or lacklustre. If you are mentally alert and concentrating, your body will be ready to react to any situation that arises. In goalkeeping there are many different aspects of the game that you have to excel at, so concentration is all the more important. It is not merely a matter of keeping your eye on the game. You must make sure you are thinking positively all the time. It is so easy to get caught flat-footed and stay on your line when you should be taking command of a situation. If your mental approach is positive, then you can tackle any problem that comes your way, otherwise you will make a mistake because your mind is wandering. That lapse in concentration could mean that you fail to go out for a cross that you could have caught comfortably. You may take your eye off a shot at the last moment and fumble it into the net. Concentration and the correct mental attitude are qualities upon which a keeper can always improve. It is something you learn and develop with experience.

In tennis and golf you often see players who have improved and, after many years, won big tournaments because their mental approach has been more positive. They have learnt from their previous mistakes. In the past, these players have been in positions to win but have not been able to manage it. When they have analysed why they didn't carry off the trophy, it is often because they were not mentally prepared.

There's many a time in goalkeeping when you have to be strong under pressure. If you are not in the right frame of mind you might make a costly mistake. Both top professionals as well as amateurs playing in weekend games for pure enjoyment want to come off the pitch feeling they have made the minimum of errors and produced some fine saves. There is a saying, which has much truth in it, that a goalkeeper is judged only on his mistakes. If he doesn't make any mistakes, critics will say he is very good. If he does not make any mistakes and produces some top-class saves, they will say he is a great goalie. If he makes good saves and several mistakes, he will be looked upon, quite naturally, as suspect. So mental approach will play a part in a goalkeeper's progress.

# 4 COURAGE

In any activity you pursue in life, and in particular in sport, you must have courage. There is the mental courage we have mentioned and physical courage. There is no point in playing any sport unless you are prepared to 'get stuck in'. There are many situations in goalkeeping where you have to show courage. You may have to risk injury diving for a ball at a player's feet, or block a thunderbolt of a shot hit straight at you from a few yards away. It also takes courage to dive among a ruck of players to take a ball in a goalmouth scramble. You never know when you are going to take a kick in the ribs or a knock on the head. They say goalkeepers have to be a little bit crazy and in many ways they are right. A keeper has to throw his body and head into dangerous

The acrobatics from Cameroon may be spectacular for those watching, but you need courage to go diving in for the ball when feet are flying.

areas among flying boots. Outfield players do not face quite the same risks. It's no use going in feet first and getting your head out of the way. By doing that you are more likely to get hurt. If you are courageous and take responsibility then you are less likely to suffer an injury.

# 5 ANTICIPATION

Anticipation is another quality you can either be born with or have to improve upon with hard work. Most keepers who have natural powers of anticipation will see dangers before they happen and be able to react early. They will always be that vital split second ahead. Anticipation means foreseeing every possible situation that may arise. You need to be able to judge shots and crosses and be one step ahead of your opponents. Be warned! I do not mean you should commit yourself too early, diving or moving before a cross comes in or a shot is struck. Once again, the mental approach is crucial, you have to be alert to move that split second earlier.

Here's an example of how a keeper can develop his anticipation. He can often assess his strategy when a midfielder plays the ball out to the wing. As the ball is being played out, a goalie can sometimes have a quick look around the penalty area to see what positions the strikers are taking up. That will give him

Good anticipation can stop a striker from latching on to a through ball and so prevent a dangerous situation for the defence.

an idea of the direction of the cross and who it may be aimed at. So a goalie can gain that vital moment's advantage when the cross is delivered. As the ball is travelling in a long pass from A to B you can take a quick glance to see how the opposition are lined up against you. Don't take your eye off the ball as a player receives it. Anticipation is the art of being able to see things that fraction of a second earlier than your opponent.

There is a new aspect of goalkeeping that has developed in the professional game which players have to be aware of, although I do not particularly agree with the practice. It is a system that has been adopted by top league clubs and teams in local football. Defences push up so far that they leave a big gap behind and the goalkeeper has to play like a sweeper, anticipating through balls over the top and race out to clear them. I disagree with the tactic because I think it stifles open football and expression, but it is a common ploy in the modern game. Indeed, this sweeper role is becoming a vital job for some goalies and is yet another situation where good anticipation is very important.

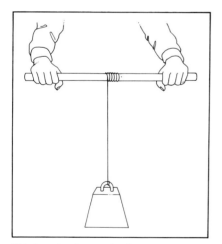

This is a simple exercise for strengthening the wrists. All that is needed is a weight on the end of a string tied to a bar. Simply turn the bar so that the weight is raised.

# 6 HANDS

Sure handling is an essential part of a goalkeeper's skills. Some players are naturally good at catching and are described as having 'good hands'. Their hands are like clamps or fly paper, the ball just seems to stick to them. Some goalies can make difficult catches with the minimum of fuss. You don't necessarily need to have enormous hands to be effective. I have seen many goalkeepers who are very clumsy at handling – although they make saves, they tend to drop, parry or knock balls away. Keepers with sound handling hold on to the ball. They take the sting out of a shot and use the shock-absorber effect I described earlier in the book.

Your wrists need to be strong and supple. Goalkeepers with weak wrists will get many injuries. You can strengthen them with a series of exercises. Strong wrists help you to hold on to the ball or deflect shots a good distance away. Both your wrists should be strong. I had mine tested on a machine recently and they were of equal strength, probably because I trained from an early age to be a goalkeeper. Exercises with weights and medicine balls can help. Hands can also be strengthened.

Perhaps one of the best examples of a goalie with good hands is the great Northern Ireland international Pat Jennings. He had enormous hands and could catch balls very easily. He could even take crosses one-handed. I would not advise you to try that, but it illustrates Pat's talent.

Balance a medicine ball in the palm of your hand. Your wrist should be bent back as shown.

As if putting a shot, straighten both your arm and your wrist.

As the ball is thrown your arm and wrist should be straight. This will help to strengthen your wrists.

# SQUARE DANCE

This is called Square Dance as the keeper has to move quickly and nimbly within a small marked-out square. It's a routine that is good for fitness, agility and footwork. Use a small area of the pitch by the corner flag for this exercise and all you need for it is a friend and a ball. You should try to build up the time you spend doing the exercise from 20 seconds' non-stop action to one minute.

**A** Staying within a ten-yard square area in the corner of a pitch, the goalie throws the ball at the server . . .

**B** . . . who deflects or knocks the ball up in the air with his hands.

**C** The keeper tries to catch the ball before it bounces.

**D** If he is unable to do this, he must catch it before the second bounce. As he gets up, the goalkeeper throws the ball back to the server, who has moved from his original position . . .

*(continued overleaf)*

**E** . . . and hits the return high or low in various directions with the palms of his hands to move the keeper around the square.

**F** The goalie may have to jump high or dive low for the ball.

# SPRINGBOARD

In this routine the keeper starts with both feet on the ground and has to spring across the goal. The exercise is designed to help footwork, speed, agility and spring. You need a full-size goal, a server and several footballs. Try ten throws at a time.

**A** The goalkeeper stands in goal a yard off the line with his back to the server. The server positions himself about seven to eight yards out in the centre of the goal.

**B** The server starts to roll the ball towards one of the corners of the net as he shouts 'Turn!'.

**C** The keeper should be in the crouched position with feet not too widely spread and turn from the hips.

**D** The goalie uses his feet quickly to get across the goal and make a save.

**E** He returns the ball to the server.

**F** The server varies the throws by changing the direction and the height.

# JUMPING BEAN

This is called the Jumping Bean as it's a fast routine forcing the keeper to jump up and down. It's a simple way of improving your spring by using the thighs and the top half of the body. All you need is a server and a football. Try to make eight to 12 catches both going backwards and forwards.

**A**  The server and keeper stand about four or five yards apart.

**B**  The server throws the ball high over the goalie's head forcing him backwards.

**C**  The keeper stretches to catch the ball. The power for the leap should come from the thighs.

**D**  He returns it to the server, who has followed the keeper . . .

**E** . . . and throws the ball again. The goalie turns his body slightly so that he is not completely face on.

**F** The keeper moves back to make another catch.

**G** The exercise is repeated with the server going backwards and the goalkeeper leaping forwards to take the ball.

# SPINNING TOP

This is an exercise that aids fitness, agility and footwork, and it is very simple to organise: all you need is a server and a football. Try to repeat it eight or ten times. Because the goalkeeper is always on the turn, this is called the Spinning Top exercise.

**A** The server stands a yard in front of the goalie, who stands in the crouched position.

**B** The server side-foots the ball through the keeper's legs. The ball should be hit between one and five yards so that the goalkeeper never knows how far he will have to dive.

**C** The keeper turns from the hips, using his feet if necessary to reach the ball . . .

**D** . . . and dives on the ball.

**E**  After making the save, he has to get up quickly.

**F**  The ball is returned to the server, who has followed the goalie, to repeat the movement. The keeper must spin alternately to his left and then to his right.

# THE YO-YO

In The Yo-Yo exercise the keeper has to dive low and spring high to get the ball. It's an excellent game to sharpen fitness and agility. For this a six-yard goal is marked out by cones. You need two servers and several footballs. Try to do 12 to 20 repetitions as fast as possible.

**A**  The keeper stands in goal with two servers facing him from about six yards. The first server throws the ball low inside the post.

**B**  The keeper dives down to stop the ball.

*(continued overleaf)*

**C** He then bounces up and returns the ball to the server.

**D** The other server throws a high ball for the keeper.

**E** The keeper catches the ball at full stretch and returns it again.

**F** Sometimes the server throwing the low balls can drop one short so the keeper has to come out.

# ZIG-ZAG LINE

In the Zig-Zag Line routine the keeper makes a scuttling run, dodging from side to side. This is good practice for moving around the goal, changing position and using feet nimbly. You need only six footballs or markers. Carry out the exercise half a dozen times going forwards and a similar number going backwards.

**A** The footballs are placed in a zig-zag pattern about two yards apart. The keeper runs up, veers to the right and bends to touch the first ball.

**B** Look up after you have touched a ball.

**C** Try to keep low as you move between the obstacles. This exercise will help strengthen your thighs.

**D** Make sure you do not cross your feet over and take as many strides as possible. Repeat the movement going backwards, remembering to keep your head and shoulders forward.

# THE QUICK STEP 1

There is a series of Quick Step exercises designed to help footwork and balance. All you need is half a dozen footballs. Do the routine six times forwards, jogging back to the starting position each time, and then six times back.

**A**  The keeper stands at the end of a line of six balls spaced about two feet apart.

**B**  The keeper runs over the top of the balls, with head and shoulders forward in a crouched position. Do this as quickly as possible with light and nimble steps. Try not to knock any of the balls.

**C**  After you have carried out the exercise a few times, try to look up as you do it.

# THE QUICK STEP 2

**A** Try the same exercise again, but this time run in and out of the six balls.

**B** Make sure your feet do not cross over or come together and, again, try to look up in between.

**C** When you get to the end of the line, attempt the same movement running backwards. Remember to keep your head forward and your knees bent.

# THE QUICK STEP 3

**A** For this Quick Step exercise move sideways over the balls.

**B** Keep in the alert position, with head forward and hands ready to make a save.

**C** Run one way leading with the right foot and then go back leading with your left.

# THE QUICK STEP 4

**A**  The final Quick Step exercise is for two-footed jumps over the balls.

**B**  Try to bounce high.

**C**  You will find this strengthens the Achilles' tendons, the ankles and calves.

# ORGANISATION

PREVIOUS PAGE: Call positively and clearly when organising your defence.

Marshalling the troops in front of him is another of the goalkeeper's responsibilities. He has to be good at organising other players, especially from any set pieces that occur in a game.

# CORNERS

It is vitally important a keeper gets his team-mates into position for a corner kick. The discipline can vary from team to team. Some managers are set in their ways on certain tactics, but at all the clubs I have played for, I have been asked how I like to set up the defence at corners. Managers have acknowledged that I know

For corners make sure that your defenders know exactly what to do and who to mark.

exactly what I want. That is not always the case, especially with less experienced players. Sometimes the boss will tell the keeper what to do.

A goalkeeper should be looking to organise his defence for corners and place players in the required positions. My personal choice is to have the two full backs on the goalposts. They provide extra insurance. If the goalie misses the cross, drops the ball, or does not punch it very far away and the ball comes back in, the full backs can often clear off the line. From any set piece, the most important point is to defend the goal first. The full backs play a big part in that. That way, if the keeper is beaten, the ball can also be stopped by the men on the line. I also like to make sure there's a man watching the near post area. I look to see that other danger positions are well covered, especially the centre of the goal and the far post. This is the basic guide for goalkeepers.

Quite often in professional football, and sometimes in local matches, an opponent will stand on the goal line, shoulder to shoulder with the keeper. I have noticed that a defender will often choose to stand with this player and mark him. That means the goalkeeper, attacker and defender are all virtually standing on each other's toes on the line. My tip for dealing with this situation is to leave the forward on his own. If a ball comes in, the keeper has to go for it whatever happens. I can tell you that it is easier to catch the ball with only one body in the way rather than having to reach over or climb above two players. It is the keeper's responsibility to take the ball in the six-yard box. I tell my team-mates to mark the strikers on the edge of or outside the six-yard box. If the opposing player who was standing on the goal line runs out into the middle of the penalty area as the ball is hit, then he's the defender's responsibility. If he stays rooted to the line as the ball comes in, then the keeper should deal with him.

One other advantage with not having a defender to mark the player on the line is that it is also much easier for referees to spot any infringements. Sometimes he can miss foul play if there is a cluster of bodies in the way. Strikers are often put in close to distract the goalkeeper going for the ball and in some cases they are used to impede him.

# FREE KICKS

When free kicks are given against his side, once again it is the goalkeeper's job to sort out the men in front of him. He has to line up defensive walls for free kicks. Some managers do not like keepers lining up the walls and leave it to an outfield player. I have always insisted on positioning the players in front of me because I feel it is my duty. However, goalkeepers can get caught out because free kicks are often taken very quickly nowadays. Opponents try to chip the ball to catch the defence unawares. If referees allow teams to take free kicks almost instantly, before the defence can be set up, it can catch goalies out.

I have always made sure that the ball cannot be bent around the outside of the wall and into the far corner of the goal from me. Having lined up the wall and moved into position, the keeper must be able to cover the ball that comes around the outside of the wall or is played over the top. There are so many brilliant strikers of the ball from free kicks that no matter what precautions you take the opposition can score. You can only carry out your own responsibilities and organise your defensive system to the best of your ability.

Free kicks hit from wide out or from beyond a shooting position can provide menacing balls centred into the box. The goalkeeper must make sure his players are picking up attackers in the correct positions. Most keepers try to use one man to cover the near post area to make sure a striker does not get in front of the defenders and get in a header. Any balls played long and over the top should be dealt with by the goalkeeper and the rest of the defence. It is not only the goalie who has a big responsibility at free kicks, the central defenders should also help to sort out the marking of the opposition.

Lining up the wall to counter a West German free kick in the semi-final of the 1990 World Cup.

# LONG THROWS

Another set piece that is prominent in professional football and becoming commonplace in local matches is the long throw. The keeper again has to make sure the players in front of him are ready to counter the threat. The main plan from a long throw is for the attacking side to get a 'flick on' header. A striker gets in front of his marker and glances the ball behind him for a second man coming in. The best way to deal with this tactic is to put an extra defender in front of the striker, so he is sandwiched between his marker and another player directly in front of him. It will now be very hard for the attacker to get a flick on. The keeper must then ensure that his defenders are not caught ball-watching as a striker could make a run and be free enough to get a flick on that results in a goal.

# FREE PLAY

The goalkeeper's organisational role extends to working closely with his defence. In most sides that comprises a back four of two centre halves and two full backs. A keeper must be the eyes in the back of the defenders' heads. The goalie is in the unique position of being able to see the whole field spread out in front of him and can help to organise positional play. You can help your back four to play the opposition offside if you feel a striker is making a run too quickly. You can also stop them dropping too far back. Sometimes defenders retreat too quickly when the opposing team are pushing forward. They get pushed back too deep and too close to the keeper. That gives him little room to work in and makes his job harder. It also leaves a great deal of space in front of the back four to be exploited by the opposing side. I don't like to see balls played up to strikers who have plenty of time and space to set up attacks.

When a cross is played into the box, the goalkeeper should have a gap between himself and his defence. This is a sort of no-man's land. When the ball is played in, a goalie has to decide whether to come out for it or whether it is his defenders' job to clear it.

A goalkeeper can be an important tactician, especially in the last third of the pitch. By good organisation, he can help the midfielders in front of the back four. He can talk to them and get the midfield and back line working together as a solid defensive barrier. The better the two units are working together the less work the keeper will have to do. If a goalie has carried out this responsibility properly he will have fewer shots to save. That is a hidden and unselfish part of goalkeeping. You can make the defence look better with your advice, organisation and encouragement. Some people will tell you after a game that you have had an easy afternoon because you have only saved a couple of shots. But they do not realise the tactical work put in by the keeper. Do not be afraid to express your opinions – too many goalkeepers notice flaws in the defence and do not say anything.

Just because a goalkeeper does a lot of shouting it does not mean he's a loudmouth. It should demonstrate that he is dominant and understands his job. Good, positive shouting goes hand in hand with organising the defence. You have to make your presence felt and your voice heard. The keeper might shout to a defender with the ball because he can see the whole pitch in front

Try to be constructive when calling to your team-mates as they may have something to say to you if you make any mistakes.

of him and realise that there is a good pass on to a player that is free. In this way he will bawl out 'left wing' or 'down the middle' to attract his attention. Always make sure the defence moves out when they clear the ball. There is nothing worse than when a defender hits the ball upfield and stands and watches. Quite often the ball comes back and the player is still standing in the 18-yard box.

Obviously, there are different types of shouts. The goalkeeper needs to be clear in the way that he calls. He can help one of his players in possession of the ball. If he sees an attacker coming in on the blind side and about to nip the ball away, he can shout 'man on'. This will give the defender an extra moment in which to release or shield the ball. He must be positive in shouting instructions to help his defenders deal with through balls played over the top. A goalie must tell his defenders to leave it or to handle the situation themselves. A quick shout will lead to decisive action and so stop misunderstandings or any hesitation. I do not like to see a keeper racing off his line and tangling with his own players because he has not called clearly and at the right moment to give the defence time to react. In hectic times these incidents can happen quite often in a game.

The tone of a goalkeeper's voice can have a big effect on his team-mates. For example, when you want a player to leave a ball for you to gather, a stern shout will get him out of the way quickly and leave him in no doubt as to your intentions. If there is plenty of time, you can call calmly and make the player realise there is no panic and he can relax. So calling is not about yelling at the top of your voice all the time. You can issue all sorts of instructions and formulate your own special calls. In this way, a good understanding can build up between you and your defenders so that they always know when you want it or when they must act quickly or when they have space to work with.

You should ensure that your calling is constructive. You need to have the respect of the other players and help them in their game. When a goalie feels let down by those in front of him, it does not hurt to give them a bit of a rollicking. That may keep the defence on its toes. However, you must avoid creating bad feeling between defenders and you – there must be respect. Always remember: a defender may have a few comments to make about you if you slip up. So make sure that when shouting you do it in the right spirit, with respect. I do not like to see players blaming each other just for the sake of making excuses.

Looking back on my first experiences of football at schoolboy level, I remember that many teachers disapproved of any player shouting except the captain. This may still be the case, but calling and communication are a big part of a keeper's game. However, players should avoid screaming and shouting at each other for the whole 90 minutes, which I am afraid is quite common in local and junior football – it is unnecessary, it is not very constructive and creates a poor team spirit. If anything goes amiss in the heat of the moment, players should shake hands and forget about it. Don't bear grudges at the end of a game. Try to see a situation from every point of view. You may have been right or wrong. So it is important to restrict the amount of shouting on the pitch and make it relevant to the job in hand.

It is worth mentioning that, in local or schools football, people and parents on the sidelines should be very wary about the type of shouting they do. There tends to be too much over-aggressive support at some matches. Families should be aware that they should encourage players and not get too carried away. It is only a game and the outcome is not a matter of life or death. Parents should realise that winning is not everything and encourage youngsters to enjoy the game.

# BLIND MAN'S BUFF

This game is called Blind Man's Buff as the keeper's view is blocked as the shot is taken. It's a good test of reactions for those times when a goalkeeper is unsighted. Once again several footballs and a goal a few yards wide are needed along with three other players. It's another routine you can keep going continually for a couple of minutes.

**A** Two players stand close together a few yards out in front of the keeper, blocking his view as the striker lines up a shot.

**B** As the striker hits the ball the players either cross over or move apart at the last moment so the keeper does not see the ball until very late.

**C** They may also deflect the ball to cause more problems.

**D** The goalie must react quickly to make a save and return the ball to the striker so the movement can be repeated.

# SKITTLE ALLEY

This exercise is called Skittle Alley as footballs will be sent flying in various directions to confuse the keeper. It's excellent practice for saving shots in a crowded goalmouth or for making saves from behind a defensive wall when late deflections can cause many problems. You need half a dozen balls and a goal five to six yards wide marked out with cones. Try to keep this routine going for a few minutes.

**A** Four balls (or cones can be used instead) are spaced evenly apart six yards from goal. The striker aims the ball towards the goal through the balls.

**B** The ball the striker kicks either goes straight through or takes a deflection.

**C** The keeper must watch carefully, and save only the ball the striker hits. Sometimes the ball will hit another and stop so the keeper has to rush out to gather it in front of goal, as if diving at someone's feet.

# PIGGY IN THE MIDDLE

This is called Piggy in the Middle and is just like the children's game, except that in this case the 'Piggy' has the advantage that he can use his hands. This exercise is played in a full-size goal. A server and two other players are needed. It's a good way of testing your judgement on crosses.

**A**  The keeper stands in his goal. A server stands ready to deliver crosses from the edge of the penalty area, close to the byline. One player stands by the near post. Another player stands level with the far post on the six-yard line.

**B**  The server varies his crosses. The keeper has to adjust his body weight either forwards or backwards and use his feet quickly to get to the ball. If he's late arriving, one of the players can head in.

**C**  The keeper moves forwards and takes the ball over the head of the player at the near post.

**D**  Here the cross has been hit to the centre of the goal. Note how I am catching the ball at full stretch to ensure no forward can head it.

*(continued overleaf)*

**E** When the ball is hit to the far post, the goalie uses small steps to cover the ground. Note how I am watching the ball all the time.

**F** The keeper makes the catch and then returns the ball to the server.

# DISTRIBUTION

Distribution is probably the most misunderstood part of the keeper's game. It is a skill that is often sadly neglected, as a goalie can add an extra dimension to the team with his creative work.

Obviously, the most important part of goalkeeping is to stop the ball going into the net, but there is more work to be done after he has made a catch or save. There is no point in making a miraculous save if you are going to give the ball back to the opposition with a bad kick or throw. Distribution is of vital importance to complete the process of stopping shots and getting your side back on the attack again. It is an art which is dying. When I started playing, keepers distributed the ball much more thoughtfully, even on local parks. There are reasons for this.

The game has changed and become more tactical. There is not so much space on the pitch, as defences tend to push out very quickly when the goalkeeper gets the ball. So there is limited room for the goalkeeper to use the ball constructively, to find a man easily and start a move. Also the new laws for keepers – the four-second rule, the number of steps allowed and the fact that he is not allowed to parry the ball down and dribble with it – have restricted his options with the ball in his hands. When the keeper could bounce the ball around in the area he had more chance to pick out a player and more scope to get into a better position to distribute the ball. Now, as soon as a goalkeeper has possession of the ball, he has to get rid of it very quickly. Often he may spot a team-mate in space on the far side of the pitch, but will not be able to get into a position to release the ball to him.

Other comparatively new tactics have altered the goalkeeper's approach to distribution. With many defences pushing up to the half-way line before the keeper kicks the ball, he's now able to dribble the ball outside the box and kick it into the last third of the opposition's half. Also, with square defences and offside tactics, a goalkeeper can sometimes deliver the ball over the opponents' defence. Keepers are taking on more and more jobs of outfield players, but this can be overdone.

In his own way, a goalkeeper can act as a playmaker, initiating moves and starting his team's attacks. Quite often a constructive throw or a well-placed kick can lead to a goal. Remember, that by using the ball sensibly, you can help your team keep possession and take much of the pressure off your colleagues.

PREVIOUS PAGE: The quick throw-out is being increasingly abandoned by keepers but it can be one of the best ways to set an attack in motion.

# THROWING

Whenever you shape up to throw, be sure you have a firm grip of the ball in your hand. Try to point your non-throwing arm at the player you are aiming for as that will help to give you good balance. Try to keep your feet apart. When you release the ball, make sure you have a good firm contact so that it will not slip out of your hands. Get your body and head in line with the target. When you release the ball, try to impart plenty of power.

A good way to practise is by throwing at a wall. Start a short distance away and practise your technique. Make a mark on the wall and try to hit it. Then gradually move backwards, increasing the distance, and try out your pace and accuracy. You can vary the trajectory, lobbing some and hurling others fast and flat like a pace bowler in cricket. When training, another useful exercise is to catch crosses and have someone in position ready to find with a throw. This makes the routine harder, because when you are catching and throwing you have two important skills of the game to think about.

One astonishing variation on the usual technique for throwing was seen during training one day at Nottingham Forest. In the other goal was recent signing Jim Montgomery, who is most famous for his heroics with Sunderland to deny Leeds United in the 1973 FA Cup final. He signalled to someone on the left that he was about to throw the ball to him, and lined up to do so. The outfield players on my team moved across to cover, but, with his eyes still focussed on the left, Jim hurled an inch-perfect pass to a player on the right who was now in acres of space. This remarkable feat is most certainly not for beginners! I have never seen anyone attempt it since.

## THROWING OUT

The underarm throw is used when you want to find one of your team-mates from a fairly close distance to set up an attack. You need to bowl or roll the ball into his path. With a well controlled roll out, the player may not even need to touch it and might be able to give a first-time pass. You would normally use the underarm throw only to team-mates nearby, like the back four or the most defensive midfield players. The overarm throw is more widely used, although it has gone out of fashion to a certain extent. That is because back fours tend to push up more and you need to throw a greater distance to find an unmarked colleague.

The underarm throw is used to pass the ball short.

In the 1970s and '80s, goalies threw the ball out far more. Then, goalkeepers used to hurl the ball high over the half-way line, instead of using a kick, as it was a more accurate means of distribution. Peter Bonetti, the former Chelsea keeper, was a master at bowling the ball out to his centre forwards' feet on the half-way line. I was always told to look first for the throw out to find a player. When that was not possible, I should then opt for a kick only as a last resort. Tactics have now changed a great deal. Keepers throw far less and kick much more. Throwing is the most accurate way of distributing the ball. It is also the safest way of keeping possession. You can hurl the ball at varying distances and heights.

When he has the ball, a goalkeeper must decide whether the player he is throwing to has time to receive, control and pass before he is challenged. You have to deliver the ball with accuracy and pace to give him as much time as possible. Try to find a colleague's feet or aim for his chest as a second option. You have to make it as easy as possible for the player to control the ball without losing possession. Once you make a save, you need good vision and awareness to pick out the unmarked player in the best position to start a move. Sometimes you can also throw into the path of a player. A good throw in space for someone to run on to can set up a good attacking situation.

# KICKING FROM HANDS

In order to be an effective kicker a keeper must be able to use both feet. Many youngsters I see tend to favour one foot only. This can be a big disadvantage. For example, you could injure your strong leg and have to use the other. Or else forwards could stand in front of you and force you to use your weaker leg. You may not be able to obtain equal strength on both sides, but you should be able to boot the ball over half-way with either foot. Make sure you get in plenty of practice with your weaker leg.

Keep your eye on the ball when kicking from the hand and don't throw it too far in front of you.

## HALF VOLLEY

This is a method a few goalkeepers like to use, but again, it is a skill that is not frequently used in the modern game. The half volley is executed by throwing the ball in the air and kicking it at the same time it hits the ground. In this way, the ball can be struck lower and often with more accuracy. With a lower trajectory, it is often easier to pick out players. When the ground is soft, be warned that this is a tricky way of distribution. There is more chance of error and especially of mishitting the ball. Opponents can score or set up goals from miscued half volleys, but if perfected it is a method of putting in an accurate long kick.

## THE VOLLEY

This is the commonest way of kicking from hands and the safest. You can be very precise with the volley, propel the ball high or low and reach players on all parts of the pitch. You can kick for accuracy by dropping the ball onto players to try to set up an attack. The other alternative is simply to go for distance and try to hammer the ball as far downfield as possible. This is a popular tactic in the modern game: defences push up and keepers aim to kick at least three-quarters of the way up the field. This can cause alarm for the defenders who have to back-pedal and get in headers. Some keepers with massive kicks can launch the ball too far and their opposite number can come off the line and take the ball. Kicks hit three-quarters the length of the field create indecision between the defence and the goalkeeper. They have to decide whose ball it is. A goalie will often not worry about accuracy when he's booting the ball long distances. He will hope his forwards can get on the end of it and cause trouble for the opposition.

When kicking from hand, it is important to get the technique right. First of all, throw the ball up well in front of you. Make sure the distance is comfortable: don't throw the ball up so close to your body that it restricts your movements, or so far away that you have to stretch to reach it. As with a golf swing, keep your head down, your eye on the ball and follow through when kicking. Sometimes you can hook or slice the ball. That happens when you have not followed the right line. Avoid throwing the ball too high as that gives more chance of an error. More follow-through will give you greater height and distance. A restricted follow-through will produce more of a punt, as it is like placing the ball on your foot.

# GOAL KICKS

There are various ways of taking goal kicks. There is the big boot over the half-way line so that strikers can challenge for the ball and gain possession. A second option is the short kick to find players around the edge of the box who could initiate a move. This brings the back four and sometimes midfielders into the game to set up moves. The keeper can also try the chipped goal kick, where he puts the ball down quickly and with very little run-up tries to loft it over the nearest opponents to find a winger or maybe a midfield player in space. This is a good ploy, but you need to be very confident to make it work. If you fluff a chip it may be cut out by the opposition. It is a highly skilful method of distribution from the floor.

Quite often in team talks I have heard managers ask a goalie how far he can kick a ball. This shows the importance managers and coaches place on distance and power. In my opinion, the length of a keeper's kicks is the least important aspect of his game.

For goal kicks, keepers must remember the golf-swing technique – eye on the ball and head down. To get more height, run up in more of an arc and try to get under the ball. If you want to impart more power, try a straighter run-up and hit right

Good balance and keeping your head over the ball are two key ingredients of a successful goal kick.

through the ball. Goalkeepers' run-ups should be well rehearsed. I always tell youngsters who have difficulty kicking off the ground to get their run-up right, get under the ball and follow through. The best advice I can give is to begin by just chipping the ball. Increase your distance as your confidence grows. You should then try to kick further and further. Do not try to kick a long distance straight away.

Weight exercises can help to add power to a keeper's kicking. Try especially to strengthen the shoulders and the thighs. Some goalies can become too muscle-bound but exercises with weights on arms and legs will produce more power.

Some keepers do not take the goal kicks for their teams, perhaps because an outfield player has an exceptionally long kick. I feel that a goalkeeper has to be in complete charge of the goalmouth and carry out every aspect of his trade. If he does not take the kicks, the opposition may feel that this is a sign of weakness. Some argue that if he fluffs a kick, he has to scurry back into goal whereas if an outfield player takes the kick, the goalie is already positioned. However, I believe that in the modern game an outfield player taking the goal kick has to rush upfield and so waste a lot of energy. Therefore a keeper should insist on taking the kicks.

Despite the latest trend for distance rather than accuracy, do not forget to work on trying to find colleagues with your goal kicks. The crowd will certainly appreciate what you are trying to do. Kicking long distances can certainly cause problems, especially as keepers can score goals. Big kicks can be carried a long way with a following wind. I once scored for Leicester against Southampton at the Dell on a wet and windy day when we were leading 4-1 with a few minutes to go. I picked up the ball and booted it down the middle. It landed right on the edge of the penalty area and the Southampton goalkeeper, Campbell Forsyth, thought a striker was going to reach the ball before him. He advanced to the penalty spot and the ball skidded wickedly off the grass, went over his head and bounced into the goal. At first, I did not realise that I had scored. In those days, we had a frantic rush after the match to catch the five o'clock train. We were in and out of the dressing room in about five minutes to reach the station on time. When my team-mates told me I'd scored, I thought they were joking. I was under the impression that Mike Stringfellow, who was chasing the ball, had put it into the net. When I got home and saw the incident on television, I had mixed feelings. First of all, it was marvellous to do something unique and score a goal, but being a member of the goalies' union I also felt a little sympathy for the Southampton keeper. I know how I would have felt if it had happened to me. So I did not take that much satisfaction from it as I knew it was a fluke. But it is pleasing to say that I have scored a goal in league soccer.

Goalkeeping is a unique position, as you can stop a goal and start a move to score one in a couple of seconds. Your awareness can catch the opposition out. If you distribute the ball quickly, they may not be well positioned in defence. Speedy clearances can create a goalscoring situation, especially after you have caught a cross. A snap throw-out can set a winger on his way, attacking the defence before they can reorganise. This is not so easy after a diving save as you have to get off the ground, but you can still catch the opposition out with a long kick downfield.

# COCONUT SHY

In this routine opposing keepers hurl the ball at each other to see who can score the most goals in this way. This is good fun and provides competition between the keepers. It's also good for fitness, speed and agility. All you need are two goals marked by cones, six yards wide and 12 to 15 yards apart. You need to work continuously for between 30 seconds and two minutes.

**A** Two goalies stand face-to-face ready for the duel.

**B** One keeper hurls the ball to try to get it past his opponent, who tries to make the save.

**C** He then gets up as quickly as possible and throws the ball back.

**D** Now it's the other keeper's turn to make a save. If you lose a ball, you must have others handy to pick up straight away.

**E** Try to vary the way you throw the ball so as to catch each other out by, for example, occasionally throwing in a high ball.

**F** The keeper then has to come out and catch it at the highest point, which is good practice for dealing with high balls into the box.

# TARGET PRACTICE

Target Practice is a good method of improving distribution. All you need is a friend, perhaps another goalie, to help you and a football.

**A** The two keepers stand 20 to 25 yards apart. Both keepers practise all their distribution techniques . . . throwing, kicking from the hand and half-volleying at their colleague.

**B** Try to aim for the feet or the chest. As each keeper gets more confident he should increase the distance.

# DISTRIBUTION 1

**A** Practise overarm throws by getting sideways on and pointing your arm in the direction you are aiming the ball.

**B** Use an action rather like a fast bowler in cricket. Note how my body weight moves from the back to the front leg as I throw.

# DISTRIBUTION 2

**A** Practise drop kicks or half-volleys by making sure you are well balanced and have your head over the ball.

**B** Make contact with the ball as it hits the ground.

**C** Follow through as you kick the ball.

# DISTRIBUTION 3

**A** Practise goal kicks by rehearsing your run-up. Approach the ball in an arc to gain more power. Youngsters should try short chips before aiming to do longer kicks.

**B** Keep your head over the ball as you make contact. Do not lean back.

**C** This is how your foot should make contact with the ball.

# DISTRIBUTION 4

**A** Practise simple side-foot passes to team-mates. Look up as you place the ball for the goal kick.

**B** Take two or three steps back. Check on your options again.

**C** Side-foot the ball accurately, keeping your head over the ball.

# PENALTIES

A penalty can often be the highlight of the game for soccer fans. It is always a tense and exciting moment – the modern-day equivalent of a duel, with one big difference (apart from a possible fatal outcome): an old-fashioned duel with pistols or swords between antagonists was an equal competition.

PREVIOUS PAGE: The penalty shoot-out at the end of the semi-final of Italia 90.

At a penalty, the odds are heavily loaded in favour of the kicker. The goalie is not expected to make a save, so he is in a 'glory to nothing' situation, but the striker is expected to score, so he is in a 'no win' position. If the keeper makes a stop he's a hero, if the kicker fails he'll feel the disappointment of his team-mates and the wrath of the supporters. It is an intriguing scenario for the goalkeeper.

Spot kicks have become more and more important in the game. Many cup-ties and tournaments are now decided by penalty shoot-outs. The idea was brought in for cup competitions to prevent a backlog of replays. I know that many people feel this is an unfair method to break the deadlock in a match, but it does provide a result and moments of high drama for the crowd. In my most memorable match, England were knocked out of the World Cup semi-finals in Italy in 1990 after a shoot-out against the

One penalty I did save against the West Germans – only it was in a friendly in 1985.

eventual winners West Germany. Perhaps it was not an appropriate way to settle such an important game, but the penalty shoot-out is now used for all sorts of local, national and international competitions.

A goalkeeper is not expected to save a kick from the spot, but I think he has a good chance of preventing the goal if he gets his technique right and is confident in his ability. Remember that the pressure is always on the striker of the ball. He is expected to score with a deadball kick in the centre of the goal from only 12 yards out. However, there is always a huge amount of tension and excitement. The opposition are usually jubilant; they feel a goal is a mere formality. There may be protests from your team-mates. So usually it takes a while for teams to settle before the kick is ready to be taken.

This time can be used profitably by the keeper. You have to realise it is your chance for a bit of glory. You must ensure that you have yourself under control, relax your mind and get your thoughts together. You must ignore all the commotion around and look to see who is taking the penalty. You might have faced him before and have an idea of his style and what he is likely to do. You need to know which foot he is liable to use before he puts the ball on the spot.

Many thoughts and ideas can be compressed into the few moments before a penalty is taken. You can gain a psychological advantage by looking cool, confident and in command. Some goalkeepers like to walk up to the ball and examine it on the spot. My advice is to get back on the line, compose yourself and get ready as the striker is placing the ball.

In some cases you can assess which side the kicker is going to try to place the ball by his run-up. When a right-footed player uses a straight run-up it is more likely he is going to place it to your left-hand side. Similarly, a left-footed player with a straight run-up is more likely to direct it to your right-hand side. If a right footer runs up in an arc, then he's probably shaping to put some pace on the ball and hit it with a full swing. In this case, the probability is the ball will go to the keeper's right. Obviously, no penalty-takers are predictable. The striker from the spot might begin his run in an arc and then come in very straight and side-foot the ball. Other penalty-takers charge in and blast the ball as hard as they can, which means they hit it high into the net. Stay as long as you can in position and don't move too early.

Some goalies make it easy for the striker by moving so early that he can virtually trickle the ball in the opposite corner to the direction of the dive. Some goalkeepers try to rush forward and then make a dive. That is ridiculous – it is difficult enough to spring across the goal without having to run forward and then change your movement. They do this because they think they are narrowing the angle. All they are doing is making it doubly difficult to make a stop. They feel they are putting off the attacker, but they are making his task much easier.

Stay on the line and try to read which direction the kick is going to go. Remain upright as long as you can. You should be moving your body a little to give you the momentum to shift your feet quickly when you have decided which way to throw yourself. Nothing looks worse than a keeper moving far too early and the ball being hit straight into the spot where he had been standing in the middle of the goal. It is surprising how many penalties are scored in this way, even in international football.

It is very difficult to get everything right when facing a penalty. The goalkeeper will rarely be blamed when a penalty is scored, except perhaps when the ball is driven straight at him or occasionally when it is a mishit that rolls in, with the keeper diving early in the wrong direction. By making that save, the goalie could win a game.

Do not be too despondent if you cannot stop a penalty. In that semi-final against Germany in the World Cup, I had the bad luck to dive the right way for four of the penalties without making a save. If the ball is hit hard and true for the corner of the net, you have little chance of reaching it, unless you move very early and the referee does not notice. You can only do your best, make a dive, trust you go the right way and hope the kick is not too hard or accurate.

Paul Cooper's remarkable penalty-saving technique works once again to deny John Robertson of Nottingham Forest in 1983.

I remember several years ago, Paul Cooper of Ipswich Town devised a method and had a great record for saving from the spot. He made his mind up to go one way and positioned himself in the goal to let the striker know which side he was going to dive. He actually waved his arms in that direction. This created confusion in the kicker's mind. He did not know whether to aim for the side Cooper was going to dive towards, where there was greater space, or to the other side where Cooper left less room. It was a difficult decision whether to hit the ball towards the large area Cooper was beckoning to or the narrower target on the other side. Penalty-takers got caught in two minds and for a while Cooper's clever ploy was a big success. Then word got around and marksmen made a decision to hit the ball decisively one way or the other. But the strategy showed that, initially, Cooper had put doubts in penalty-takers' minds. This shows the mental side of penalty-taking under pressure.

Goalkeepers can often play a bluff when facing a penalty. Some keepers move the top half of their body a great deal to look as though they are going one way. They pretend to move left and dive right. The fascinating aspect of dealing with penalties is that, with experience, goalkeepers can develop their own techniques.

# PINBALL

We call this game Pinball, because the ball ricochets around the goalmouth. It's another exercise designed to help your reactions. It also teaches keepers to stand up until the last possible moment and change direction quickly. Once again you need a goal marked out by cones five to six yards wide, several footballs, a server and two other players.

**A** For this routine the server stands about ten yards in front of the goal, facing the keeper, with a player standing just outside each post.

**B** The server will dictate where the ball goes and hit it towards one of the players, who can deflect the ball towards the goal off their feet, head, chest or any part of their body.

**C** The ball can be played between the two players for variation.

**D** The keeper must react quickly to make a stop and return the ball so the exercise can be repeated.

# SHOOT-OUT

Shoot-out is a short penalty competition. It is excellent practice for standing up as long as possible before committing yourself to the dive and then getting down to save shots. All you need is a goal five yards wide marked by cones, a server and a number of footballs. Try facing 10 to 20 shots.

**A** The keeper crouches in the ready position. The server stands a yard away from the ball just eight yards out.

**B** The server puts in a quick shot and tries to send the goalkeeper the wrong way.

**C** The keeper must get down fast to make the save.

**D** The goalie must stand up until the last possible moment and not try to guess which way the ball will go.

*(continued overleaf)*

**E** The striker should aim either side so that the keeper can practise diving both ways.

**F** Obviously, this will give both players a chance to develop their penalty skills and compete. However, the server should place the shots, trying to deceive the goalkeeper rather than blasting away at him.

# TRAINING

There have been many innovations in goalkeeper training over the last few years. The way keepers work out and develop their skills has improved radically over the last 20 years. Managers and coaches have finally realised that it is a position that requires specialised training.

PREVIOUS PAGE: In training for England. Similar exercises are shown above (*see* page 102-04).

In my opinion, the correct training and preparation are essential in any sporting career. There are those who are naturally gifted at a certain sport and develop skills without any need to practise. Whatever the level of your natural ability, good training will help to enhance your skills. If a talented player does not work at his game and a less talented individual trains thoroughly, the gap in ability between the two will diminish. It is most important to have the right attitude towards training. Some players and teams approach the job without any thoughts and plans. You should know what you are doing and why. Training should be enjoyable as well as beneficial.

It is only by practice and repetition that you can develop a technique that will stand up in a match situation. In many cases in professional sport, when the pressure is on, this is when the skills perfected in training will hold you in good stead. Long hours spent on the training ground can pay dividends.

Training with Chris Woods for England. It is very important to practise in a constructive manner.

The art of goalkeeping is fascinating because there are so many aspects of the game that need to be right. You must always strive to improve and make sure there are no weaknesses in any part of your game. Look at all the components of the keeper's job and try to work on your weaknesses as well as on your strengths. Put in more time on aspects of the game in which you lack confidence. If you have a problem, keep working at it; don't be despondent. With hard work, it will eventually come right. Find out the right technique and keep rehearsing it.

When you have plenty of time to make a stop or take a cross, you can get away with poor technique. It is when you are under pressure and have little time to react that bad habits can lead to basic mistakes. Good training helps to eliminate risks in a match, so you will benefit from all your work on the practice ground.

A goalkeeping coach will obviously be helpful in giving you the right guidance. If you have no access to a coach, try to tailor your training to your personal needs. If you want to practise stopping certain types of shots, get your friends to fire a barrage of them at you. Everyone will benefit; they practise their shooting and you practise making saves. I used to write down training exercises and try them out with my friends. You can help other players with their skills – for example, you can throw the ball out for them to chest down or help in an exercise when players are pushing over centres for heading practice. It is particularly important that youngsters work together to improve their game. Try out tactics and ideas with your pals in the local park. If you're missing crosses, get two or three friends to pump over a stream of them for you to catch. When you next play in a match, you will find that your technique has improved in certain situations because of the work you have put in during training.

As I explained earlier in the book, I always liked playing in the outfield in some games as a youngster just in case I did not make it as a keeper. I still like a run-out in training, as I feel it is important to gain an appreciation of the forward's job. You can also get an insight into what goes through a striker's mind. It is a good experience to try other positions and also provides a little extra fun and enjoyment.

The correct preparation is important for training as well as for matches. You need to get the right amount of sleep and rest. You should also be careful with your diet and intake of liquid. Do not eat just before you go out to train. That can make you feel ill. Ideally, you need to eat three hours before doing any vigorous exercise so that food is properly digested. It is necessary to eat enough to provide the fuel to give you the required energy for your work. It is also vital to take in a lot of liquid before and after training to make sure you replace the body fluids you lose. You should avoid taking too much out of yourself if you have not put enough in. Your body is rather like a machine or an engine – it needs oil to keep it working and petrol for fuel. In the same way, you need food and liquid.

The right amount of rest is also necessary. Try to relax before and after training, as that will maximise the benefit of the session.

Mental preparation is important for training as well as for matches. When you go on the pitch, you must be in a positive frame of mind. Join in enthusiastically with the exercises the coach devises. I have always stayed after training for specialist sessions. Try not to practise skills of the game, like heading, that are of no use to you when you can do essential goalkeeping work. There is a balance to achieve in your mental approach. Try to relax but get into a winning mood. Develop a will to keep the ball out of the net and this can help your team-mates. Banish all negative thoughts from your mind before training and games. Do not get too tensed up.

Getting used to strange conditions is a vital part of match preparation. The World Cup squad of 1986 went to Colorado Springs before going on to Mexico.

It may not be fun to train in the rain – but if you do not do so you'll not be used to the conditions when it pours down in a match.

I always advise goalkeepers to train in all conditions and on every surface. It is very important to train in wet and windy weather. You may get soaked and feel uncomfortable, but it is important to get used to the slippery ball and the wind blowing crosses and shots. Similarly, you should be willing to train in icy and snowy conditions. In the depths of winter you may have to play in that sort of weather.

Be extra careful when training on hard surfaces, as they may cause bad bruises or more serious injuries. Do as much work as you can on different surfaces. For example, when it is dry and hard, the ball will bounce slower than when there's a firm surface with a little dew and you need to get used to these variations.

A goalkeeper must maintain the balance of being a part of a team, in terms of training, as well as being an individual in a specialised position. It is enjoyable working with a squad of players in training. You can enjoy a bit of friendly competition. You should avoid becoming too obsessive or too much of a loner in the side.

# ROLLER BALL

Roller Ball is a simple way of getting in some catching practice on your own. The exercise helps handling and reactions. All you need is a football and a heavy pitch roller.

**A** Stand about six yards in front of the roller and volley the ball at it.

**B** The curve of the roller will make the ball rebound at different angles.

**C** Sometimes the ball will bounce high off the top of the roller . . .

**D** . . . and the keeper will have to spring to make a catch.

**E** When it is kicked lower, the ball may drop short . . .

**F** . . . so the goalie then dives forward to pounce on the short ball.

# SKID ROW

Skid Row is an exercise that will be of great value when a keeper has to deal with shots on a wet and slippery surface during a match. It teaches the goalie how to get his feet out of the way quickly and to get body and head behind the ball. The keeper also has to keep his eye on the ball in case it bounces awkwardly. Once again, a goal five yards wide is required, plus the help of a server armed with a pile of footballs.

**A** The server faces the keeper from about eight yards.

**B** The server bowls the ball overarm as fast as possible to make the ball skid through.

*(continued overleaf)*

**C** He bounces some deliveries just in front of the keeper.

**D** Others are bounced shorter to make the ball rear up.

**E** The keeper has to make a catch . . .

**F** . . . and returns the ball to the server.

# GYM EXERCISE 1

This series of exercises is for general strength and fitness. All you need is a trainer or friend to help you, and a ball. All the exercises can be done either outside or in the gym. This one will strengthen your legs and stomach.

**A** The keeper and trainer stand about six to eight yards apart.

**B** The coach throws a high ball . . .

**C** . . . and the keeper has to leap two-footed to make a catch.

**D** He returns the ball to the trainer and falls down into a press-up position.

**E** The goalie does a press-up and then, as he stands up, the coach throws the ball.

# GYM EXERCISE 2

This exercise helps to stretch and strengthen the upper half of the body.

**A** The coach stands with a ball in his outstretched hands. The keeper lies flat out with his feet in between the coach's legs and his arms behind his head.

**B** The goalkeeper has to sit up and touch the ball, but his legs must stay straight. He then goes back to the starting position.

**C** The trainer holds the ball at different heights and angles to vary the body movement.

# GYM EXERCISE 3

This is an exercise that stretches and strengthens back muscles. Repeat about ten times.

**A** The keeper lies flat out on his stomach. The trainer faces him a few yards away and rolls the ball quickly towards him.

**B** The keeper makes a stop on the ground . . . .

**C** . . . and arches his back and legs, ready to throw the ball.

**D** He throws the ball back to the trainer to repeat the movement. The distance can be increased as the keeper gets stronger.

# GYM EXERCISE 4

This exercise can be repeated ten times. It is excellent for stretching and strengthening the back.

**A** The keeper lies on his back with his legs bent and hands behind his head. The trainer stands over him, holding a ball level with the top of the keeper's knees.

**B** The keeper arches his back and touches the ball with his stomach. He holds the position for a few seconds and then relaxes. The trainer can hold the ball lower to start with and gradually increase the height when the keeper improves at the exercise.

# GYM EXERCISE 5

This is a good work-out for two-fisted punching practice and toning stomach muscles. The movement can be repeated ten times.

**A** The server stands three yards away from the keeper. The keeper lies flat on his back with his hands stretched out behind his head.

**B** As the server throws the ball, the keeper sits upright, but his legs must stay on the floor. He should bring his fists together as he does so, and not use his hands to push himself up.

**C** The goalie punches the ball two-handed back to the server for the exercise to carry on. As the keeper gets stronger, the coach can move further back.

# EXTRAS

# ROUTINE

In football, a well-established pre-match routine can be very important to prepare a player for a game. Managers often have very different ideas. Some like to talk to players and brief them thoroughly about a forthcoming game the day before. Others only mention the match strategy just before kick-off.

You should be able to prepare yourself for a game by finding the routine that suits you best. On match days I like a lie in, but not for too long. I usually wake up before nine o'clock then rest for at least another half an hour. After breakfast I go for a walk for about 20 minutes to get some fresh air. Players usually eat three hours before a game to make sure their food is digested. You need to eat something light. I always have a plate of baked beans and scrambled eggs. Other players prefer pasta, cornflakes and peaches or just toast and tea.

After the pre-match meal I try to relax by watching television. We usually report for the game about an hour and a quarter before kick-off. I like to check on my kit and make sure my gloves do not have any splits. Other players use the time to put on strappings or rub in some oils or linament. In the ten minutes or so before we go out onto the pitch, I like to sit down and relax. Some players like to jump up and down, talk loudly and shout to each other, but I don't like to get too excited. I prefer to remain calm before going out to perform.

After matches, most players like to have a night out. In my early days I would do the same. I now prefer a night in, relaxing with the family over a takeaway meal. In Italy and several other continental countries, players are advised to rest after a game and not go out on the town. The idea is that they should let their bodies recover after all the exertion. That approach may well come to this country.

For amateur players, the match-day routine may not be so easy. For instance, you may have to work before a game. The most important thing to remember is to eat well before the start and try to get some rest and relaxation before the kick-off.

# CAPTAINCY

One of my proudest memories was captaining England. I savoured every moment that I led my country in international football, but despite this I do not believe a keeper is the best man to skipper a side. After my experiences, I would say a goalie is

Leading out the England side was a great honour for me. Here we take on Australia in June 1983 at one of the more picturesque stadiums I have ever played in.

quite a good choice to captain his country, but certainly not the ideal player to lead a club side.

I am not totally against a goalkeeper taking charge of a team, I just feel that it is a job that can be performed better by an outfield player. For example, at club level you get many young players making their debuts and an outfielder is in a better position to talk to them and give advice and it would be hard for a keeper to do that. There might be several inexperienced players in a side who need nursing along. It is much easier for a goalkeeper to lead an international side. At that level, captaincy is more a case of prestige. I think it is fair to say that directing operations is not nearly as hard when you are surrounded by the country's most talented and experienced performers. There's a famous old saying that a good team has 11 captains on the field and I have played in international sides that have contained four or five players who have led out their clubs.

There is a theory that being in goal is a perfect position from which to lead a side. Some people say a keeper can see the whole match taking shape in front of him. There is a certain amount of truth in that but, as I have explained, the lines of communication are very difficult. As well as the problem of guiding young players, a goalie would find it very hard to have a word with his strikers in the heat of the battle. There have been some very successful goalkeeper/captains, however. Mark Wallington led my old club Leicester. Martin Hodge took charge at Sheffield Wednesday and Dave Beasant captained Wimbledon to their FA Cup success in 1988. Also, remember that Dino Zoff led Italy to World Cup triumph in Spain in 1982 at the age of 40.

I have mentioned before that a keeper is a bit of a loner and is in a highly specialised position. He requires 100 percent concentration and the responsibilities of captaincy can be distracting. A goalkeeper has to perform as a type of captain in any case and command his penalty area and defence.

Captaining England was a great thrill, and I am proud of my record. I led out England ten times before ending on the losing side. That was against Argentina in the quarter-finals of the 1986 World Cup in Mexico . . . Beaten by the hand and foot of Maradona.

Marco van Basten may be one of the greatest strikers in Europe, but there's no time to worry about a forward's reputation when he's closing in on goal.

# REPUTATIONS

The saying that reputations count for a lot is not completely true in soccer. I have heard radio and TV commentators say that some striker has delayed his shot or was put off by the presence of a famous goalie. Top strikers are not daunted by the keeper they are up against. Don't imagine for a moment that Ian Rush, Gary Lineker or Dean Saunders will hesitate or fret when they have to beat a top international goalkeeper. That probably makes them all the more determined as they will take even more credit for beating a top-class keeper. Similarly, a goalkeeper should not be in awe of famous sharp-shooters. The exception to this may be when a player from the lower leagues comes up against a top-class goalie. In these cases, I have often noticed that strikers are inclined to try too hard and maybe tense up. In trying to put the ball right in the corner, they might miss the target.

The right image can even be of benefit to a keeper in building his reputation. I mentioned the great Russian star Lev Yashin. He dressed in all black and created a presence that made him look strong and unbeatable. I always admired him, but generally reputations count for nothing when a match gets under way. The only way you will put pressure on opponents and stop shots is through superior technique and, of course, a little bit of good fortune too.

# KIT

The selling and promotion of football gear is a rapidly expanding business. At the start of every season, parents and youngsters rush into the sports shops to buy their club's latest strip or colours. The huge choice of soccer kit can be overwhelming. All sorts of styles and designs are available.

I have to say that one of the biggest changes in my career is the strip I now put on to play in goal. When I started in the early 1960s, boots had toe caps and you had to nail the studs into the sole. They used to come up above the ankle like rugby boots. In those days, my boots were my pride and joy; I used to clean and polish them and cover them with dubbin to make them look like new. My first jerseys were made out of wool and had a roll neck. They became very heavy when it was wet as they soaked up all the moisture. I also wore longer shorts made out of a heavier material.

The shirt was plain and the gloves were woollen in this 1974 international against Scotland . . .

There were no such things as goalkeeping gloves. Keepers used to wear string ones, although a cotton glove was developed for goalkeepers later in the 1960s. I first saw special goalkeeping gloves, made of leather, when I went on a youth club trip to Germany. I bought a pair, but found them a bit slippery for catching the ball and went back to using string gauntlets. The Germans in particular led the way in developing a range of goalkeeping gloves.

The type of football that I used as a lad now looks like something out of a museum. It was made of heavier leather, with very prominent panelling and was laced up around the valve where it was pumped up. The balls in those days did not have a waterproof plastic coating. When it was wet, they soaked up all the moisture and became very heavy – I even saw players knocked out by heading the ball because it was such a weight. When you played in goal, you had to get both hands behind it or else you could easily be injured.

Nowadays, there is an enormous variety of boots. Some have moulded studs and others have different types of screw-in studs. The modern shoe can be very light and is cut very far below the ankle. It is up to the individual to decide what boot suits him best and feels most comfortable. It is more important to choose the most suitable studs for the conditions you are going to play in. No

. . . but a goalkeeper's kit has come a long way since then. The elbows and shoulders are padded, while the gloves ensure that a keeper can hold on to the ball more easily. But never forget that good kit does not make a good goalie.

matter how fit you are, if you are going to slip and lose your footing in a game you will have problems. Look through the brochures and make sure you have the right studs for the day. Obviously, you will need longer studs for muddier pitches and shorter ones for harder grounds.

I am a great believer in always wearing shin pads. There are now many different types available. Some have built-in ankle straps as part of the pad. I prefer this type as it gives extra protection and stops cuts and bruises on the ankle. Remember that wearing shin pads could prevent a very serious injury that could put you out of the game for weeks or months.

If you look through the catalogues in a sports shop, you will see a wide range of goalkeepers' jerseys. There are so many colours and patterns, as well as various materials for different conditions. Simply find a jersey you like. My preference is to wear one with padded elbows and shoulders.

There are all sorts of extra strappings and padding available for keepers such as thigh strappings and knee and elbow pads. I don't wear these, but they can be useful to protect an injury. If you wear ankle strappings in a game, then do not use them in training, as that can weaken your ankles.

A wide choice of gloves is now available. New technology has developed gauntlets for dry and wet weather. Be careful not to wear dry weather gloves when it is pouring with rain as the ball will slip out of your hands.

Another useful item of kit is a glove bag. You may need to change gloves if conditions alter during a match or if you split one of them. You can also put some useful items inside a glove bag. A cap may be needed if the sun is in your eyes, but I never wear one unless the glare is really unbearable. Extra tie-ups are another item to keep handy. Some keepers put lucky charms in their glove bag, but I do not believe in that. Other goalies like to chew gum, but that is something I do not recommend as gum can easily get stuck in your throat, which can be very dangerous. As the main purpose of the gum is to keep your mouth moist, it is a far better idea to put a small carton of soft drink in your bag and have a quick sip if there's a long hold-up in play.

In this country, keepers generally wear the same shorts as the rest of the team. On the continent, longer ones are currently in fashion. Goalkeepers often wear tight-fitting shorts that stretch down to the knee, sometimes padded.

There are now special tracksuits for keepers. Some of these have knee and side padding, which is helpful when you are training on hard ground. There are waterproof suits for soggy conditions, so you do not feel wet and miserable during a long training session.

When selecting any kit do not pay any attention to the maker's name and design. Buy the gear that feels most comfortable and suitable for you. Youngsters often save up for months to buy soccer equipment and parents are always having to dip into their pockets to buy kit. Try to buy what you can afford and do not overstretch yourself. An important point to remember is that the most expensive articles are not necessarily the best. You will be judged on your ability and not on the value of your strip. If you are decked out in the most expensive gear, it won't make you a better player.

What is far more important is to see young players smartly turned out in their soccer kit. Never go onto the field in dirty boots and clothing. If you are playing in a Sunday friendly, a local league or the First Division you should take pride in your appearance. If your kit is immaculate, that will be reflected in your performance. Kit may be expensive, but it does not cost much to make sure your clothing is clean and well ironed and your boots polished and shiny.

# PICTURE CREDITS

All the exercise pictures used throughout the book were taken by Andrew Cowie of Colorsport, to whom the author and the publishers are greatly indebted.

Action Images: 73, 108, 110
Action Plus: 106
All-Action Pictures: 90
All-Sport: 105 (Simon Bruty), 157
Apex: 7, 83, 151
Neville Chadwick: 29
Colorsport: 24, 25, 26, 31, 32, 38, 40, 41, 43, 47, 63, 66, 68, 85, 89, 117, 132, 140, 156
Empics: 27, 121
Professional Sport: 120, 123, 139, 154
Peter Shilton: 19, 20, 22, 23
Split Second: 131
Sporting Pictures: 46
Bob Thomas Sports Photography: 9, 11, 13, 30, 35, 44, 65, 87, 134, 142, 143, 153

# ACKNOWLEDGEMENT

I would like to thank Dennis Coath for all his help in putting together this book.

**Peter Shilton**